# The SCANDALOUS LIVES of CAROLINA BELLES

## Marie Boozer
### and
## *Amelia Feaster*

# The SCANDALOUS LIVES of CAROLINA BELLES

## Marie Boozer and Amelia Feaster

*FLIRTING WITH THE ENEMY*

TOM ELMORE

THE History PRESS

Published by The History Press
Charleston, SC 29403
www.historypress.net

Copyright © 2014 by Tom Elmore
All rights reserved

First published 2014

ISBN 978-1-5402-2456-9

Library of Congress CIP data applied for

Portions of this book previously appeared in "Lurid Legends of a Wayward Woman," which was published in *Civil War Magazine* in August 1997.

*Notice*: The information in this book is true and complete to the best of our knowledge. It is offered without guarantee on the part of the author or The History Press. The author and The History Press disclaim all liability in connection with the use of this book.

All rights reserved. No part of this book may be reproduced or transmitted in any form whatsoever without prior written permission from the publisher except in the case of brief quotations embodied in critical articles and reviews.

*To my parents,*

*Roy and Connie Elmore,*

*for giving me a love of books and history.*

# Contents

| | |
|---|---|
| Acknowledgements | 9 |
| Introduction | 11 |
| 1. Early Life | 15 |
| 2. The Civil War Years | 25 |
| 3. Up North | 41 |
| 4. The Countess de Pourtalès | 55 |
| 5. Legends and Lies | 65 |
| Notes | 89 |
| Bibliography | 103 |
| Index | 109 |
| About the Author | 111 |

# Acknowledgements

I am indebted to the following people and institutions for helping make this book possible:

Kent Book, librarian, Union League of New York, for answering my requests of information.

Dr. Chester DePratter of the South Carolina Institute of Archaeology and Anthropology for sharing some valuable leads.

Chad Rhoad of The History Press for having the patience of Job.

The South Carolina Confederate Relic Room and Military Museum, Columbia, South Carolina, for allowing the use of the images of Camp Sorghum and Camp Asylum.

The South Carolina Department of Archives and History, Columbia, South Carolina.

The South Caroliniana Library of the University of South Carolina–Columbia, in particular, Graham Duncan.

The Southern Historical Collection of the Wilson Library at the University of North Carolina at Chapel Hill.

The Walker Family and Local History Research Center at the Richland County Public Library, Columbia South Carolina, for the use of several images.

Civil War historian Eric Wittenberg for sharing with me a letter to Amelia Feaster.

Mr. James Young of sc-families.org.

Speedy and Sassy for protecting me from nasty noises.

## Acknowledgements

My mother-in-law, Pat Wood, for looking over and proofreading the text for me.

My wife, Krys, for her cheerleading, editing, patience and love.

And last but not least, Marie and Amelia for leading such interesting lives and giving me my start as a published writer.

# *Introduction*

[Marie Boozer was] *one to be spoken* [of] *in whispers but never, oh never, out loud.*
Elizabeth Boatwright Coker[1]

We live in a celebrity-obsessed world, constantly bombarded by supermarket tabloids, entertainment news shows, websites and "reality" series, many of which are devoted to people who are famous only for being famous. This is not a new phenomenon; in the nineteenth century, people visited wax museums or magic lantern shows to see images of the famous (or infamous) people of the day. Similar gratification could be found in the spoofs of celebrities performed in burlesque, music hall and vaudeville shows, or you could see their lives re-created in melodramas.

Or for those with a literary bent, there were dime novels containing exaggerated or fabricated tales of such men of action as William "Buffalo Bill" Cody. There was also the popular *National Police Gazette*, which lured readers with shocking stories of murders, outlaws and sex scandals, accompanied by drawings of skimpily clad strippers, burlesque performers and prostitutes.

And for those nineteenth-century Americans with a taste for sensationalism, there was the yellow press, which relied on scandalous headlines and newspaper stories with little, if any, legitimate research, using instead gossip, scandals or exaggerations to back their claims. For this ilk, Marie Boozer and her mother, Amelia Feaster, were the perfect subjects.

When reviewing their lives, one can see a number of similarities between Marie and Amelia and Kim Kardashian and Kris Jenner. Both mothers

## Introduction

have shamelessly self-promoted their daughters and ridden on the coattails of their daughters' to fame. Both young ladies have been linked to famous and wealthy men and have been the subject of endless gossip. But try to ask someone on the street how these women became so famous, and the most likely answer you would get is, "I don't know."

While some of Kim and Kris's fame has come from their television shows, Marie's is a little harder to figure out. She never fired a gun in battle or served in combat during the Civil War. There is no evidence that she even served as a spy. In fact, the only contribution we can safely say Marie made to the Civil War effort was to volunteer as a nurse. However, during the war and for decades afterward, Marie was a popular subject of gossip, books and magazine articles. Had the *National Enquirer* or *TMZ* existed in the late nineteenth century, she would have been featured regularly.

I first came to know of Marie back in the early 1990s while researching my book *A Carnival of Destruction: Sherman's Invasion of South Carolina*, though I had been aware of her existence since the late 1970s, when my mom brought home a copy of *La Belle*, a novel loosely based on Marie's life. Though at best a minor figure of the war, her name kept popping up in more places than I ever would have expected and was written about more than some Civil War generals. Consequently, I started collecting her stories and, eventually, put them together in the first magazine article I ever sold: "Lurid Legends of a Wayward Woman" for *Civil War Magazine* in August 1997. This was the most accurate and fact-based account of her life ever published until now. To this day, I still keep a framed image of her on my wall out of gratitude.

Since the publication of that article, I have continued to collect information about her life. Thanks to the Internet and the proliferation of genealogy websites, more information about Marie has surfaced, filling in many of the gaps in her story.

Originally, my plan was to do an updated version of the 1997 piece as an appendix in *Carnival*. However, at the last minute, due to lack of space, I removed the update and replaced it with an all-too-brief recap of Marie's life in the main text.

In retrospect, I made the right call. People as colorful as Marie and Amelia deserve their own biographies. Thus, almost twenty years after I started my "romance" with Marie, I find myself revisiting her, still trying to present the most complete and accurate account of her and her mother's lives.

However, I must offer this caveat: so much of their lives are still shrouded in mystery, legend and gossip that we will probably never learn all the details of them, in particular, the early years of Amelia Sees Harned Burton Boozer

## Introduction

Feaster and Marie's biological father, Peter Burton. Yet after sorting through the half-truths, legends and the all-too-few verifiable bits and pieces, a nineteenth-century tale that rivals any modern tabloid story has emerged.

In addition to recounting the lives of Marie and Amelia, I have also included a chapter on how the legend of Marie has grown over the course of 135 years, not unlike Dr. Seuss's "plain horse and wagon" on Mulberry Street becoming a big parade. This is a fascinating tale on its own and explains how Marie became incorrectly associated with so many misadventures.

As you read this, there is one thing to keep in mind. It has been said that true beauty is something that is unforgettable. By an interpretation of that standard, Marie Boozer is a true beauty, as the name of the Confederacy's femme fatale still graces the pages of history texts and the collective memory of many in the city of Columbia.

# CHAPTER 1
# *Early Life*

The tale of two of the Confederacy's most infamous women begins north of the Mason-Dixon line in Philadelphia, Pennsylvania. There on January 30, 1819, Amelia Sees, the seventh of nine children and one of six daughters, was born to George Sees Jr. (1781–1835) and Mary Carr (1787–1871), who were of French Huguenot descent.[2]

One writer described Amelia as follows:

> *One of the most beautiful women we have ever met; her complexion was faultless, her eyes large, dark and brilliant, and her hair (which was very abundant) was black as the raven's wing and glossy as satin; her forehead was broad and high, indicating the intellect she certainly possessed; her pearly teeth and scarlet lips completed the loveliness of her face. She was exceedingly graceful and dangerously fascinating, possessing also rare conversational power; with her "to will was to do."*[3]

He went on to say, "If she made up her mind to captivate man, woman or child, it was useless to resist—the only safety was in flight."[4]

Another writer described Amelia as "one rich, dark in coloring and costume." Intellectually, Amelia was considered a "very smart woman and not over-scrupulous," who "in the time of trouble looked ahead."[5]

She apparently had no scruples when it came to lying about her age. The 1850 U.S. census lists Amelia as twenty-five, while the 1860 census lists her as only thirty.[6]

Amelia Feaster. This pre–Civil War image is the only known likeness of this real life jezebel. Sadly, there are no known photographs of any of her husbands. *Author's collection.*

The first two decades of Amelia's life are almost a complete mystery. Supposedly at age fifteen, she married a man named Henry or Thomas Harned, but the only thing known about this union is that her husband died the day after the wedding.[7]

In fact, Amelia disappears from the public record until 1841, when she married Peter Burton of Columbia, South Carolina, in Charleston, South Carolina. Allegedly, she met Burton while he was on a buying trip to Philadelphia for his employer, a dry goods merchant. Burton, who "was not attractive or brilliant," was introduced to Amelia as a rich merchant. Tradition holds that he was much older than she was.[8]

Peter and Amelia's wedding was officiated by the Reverend William C. Davis and was probably held at the Third Presbyterian Church in Charleston, South Carolina.[9]

The Burtons' marriage lasted only two years, but it did produce one child, Mary Adele Peter Burton, presumably named after Amelia's mother. Fittingly, we are not certain when Marie was born. Many accounts say she was born in 1846, but this is based on the writings of an early biographer, Julian Selby, who actually stated that she was born "*about* the year 1846 [emphasis added]." Selby was deliberately vague because he did not "consider it polite to be too explicit as to the year and month" of Marie's birth.[10]

The 1860 U.S. census lists Marie as thirteen on July 18, meaning she was born in 1846 or 1847. Even Marie's own family was uncertain. A half sister claimed that Marie's birth date was February 28, 1848, but a stepfather said the family Bible had it as February 28, 1850. It is this last date that Marie herself probably accepted, as it conforms to her obituaries.[11]

Another subject of controversy concerning Marie is the correct spelling of her name. While some writers use "Mary," many others use "Marie." Her legal birth name is spelled "Mary" in the 1860 census, though she pronounced it "Marie." Furthermore, a post–Civil War photograph of hers is signed "Mary Boozer." However, by the 1870s, she was spelling her name "Marie."[12]

## Early Life

Burton died prior to 1847, supposedly four months after the birth of Marie, which, if true, means that Marie never got to know her biological father, while also confirming her birth year as 1846. According to an account written by someone identified only as C.D.M., Burton "died a mysterious death in which there were hints of murder." After Burton's death, Amelia supported herself as a dressmaker.[13]

Amelia soon married her third husband, David Boozer, from Newberry, South Carolina. On an Easter holiday to Newberry, Amelia had planned to stay at the Birdsfield Hotel, which Boozer owned, but it was closed due to renovations. Consequently, Boozer, who had met Amelia in Columbia before, took her in at his house.[14]

Amelia and David were married in 1847 at Avaleigh Presbyterian Church by Reverend E.F. Hyde. "Big Dave," as Boozer was affectionately called, was born in 1788 and came from German ancestry. He was a widower and the owner of a large farm in addition to the hotel.[15]

The Boozers lived in the town of Newberry, South Carolina, the county seat of Newberry County. The county had a population of 20,143 people in 1850 and was largely farmland, with cotton and corn being the two most common crops. The town of Newberry itself, one resident observed, "extends

The restored Newberry downtown area looks similar today as it did when Amelia lived there. *Photograph by the author.*

a mile, every way, from the court house, and I hope, in less than five years, all this space will be fully occupied, by an active enterprising population. The streets are entirely too narrow, being only 33 feet wide."[16]

As his first wife, Sarah Suber (1786–1840), left Boozer with no children, he legally adopted Marie, rechristening her Mary Sarah Amelia Boozer, after his first and second wives.[17]

Attorney John Belton O'Neall had known Boozer since 1808 and, in his 1859 book, *The Annals of Newberry*, wrote that Boozer "was possessed of great energy of character; had generally a great flow of spirits, and until within a few years had been attended by unexampled prosperity."[18]

However, after Boozer's marriage to Amelia, things started going bad financially for Big Dave, and his personality took a dark turn. O'Neall wrote, "Although he was still surrounded by an ample estate," Boozer's financial misfortunes "unsettled his reason, and led to the rash, mad act, which he committed." On February 10, 1850, Boozer shot himself in the head in his coach house with a double-barrel shotgun, blasting away the upper part of his head.[19]

O'Neall, who was the executor of Boozer's estate, lamented:

> *He left a widow, his second wife, and an adopted child to mourn their great loss. His aged mother, of more than four score years, still survives; sad and awful indeed was it to see her bending over his mangled remains, and lamenting her first born son only as a mother can lament. He was an honest, good man. How frail, however, is poor humanity, at all times, and never more sadly illustrated than in the case of David Boozer's suicide.*[20]

Boozer's will left instructions for Amelia to use the proceeds from his estate to care for and educate Marie and that, upon Amelia's death, the entire estate would be given to Marie. Marie also inherited an elderly slave couple, Stobo and Hannah, with whom she enjoyed a close bond, and the couple's two children, Lizzy and William. According to one account, the value of Marie's share of the estate was $25,000, though another suggests that it was worth only $9,904.[21]

David Boozer was buried in the old Aveleigh Presbyterian Cemetery in Newberry. In his will, he left very specific instructions for his final resting place.

The testator directed his executors

> *to enclose a grave-yard at Aveleigh Church, from 45 to 50 yards square, with a wall of split rock from 4½ to 5 feet high, so as to enclose the grave of my first*

*wife, as well as my own, with sufficient space also for the grave of my present wife; and to erect over the area included by the wall, a covered wooden building of the most lasting materials, to be finished and painted in appropriate style, and in the most durable manner. And I appropriate one thousand dollars out of my estate to these purposes:—Held, that the grave-yard intended to be enclosed and covered was one of forty-five or fifty square yards.*[22]

This part of the will was challenged by Amelia in the courts. The judge in the case ruled that "an area of 45 or 50 *yards square* could not be enclosed with stone and covered by a wooden building for less than $4,600; and that an area of 45 or 50 *feet square* could be enclosed and covered as directed by the will for $900 or $1,000 [emphasis added]." Furthermore it was argued that "a structure sufficiently extensive to cover three graves is frequently found within rural grave-yards; but one large enough to cover 45 or 50 yards square, or half an acre, is without' example; it would be most ungainly, and would exhaust, several times over, the amount of the fund appropriated." Consequently, he ruled that the will be modified to replace the term "yards square" to "square yards," thus allowing a smaller burial plot.[23]

In 1935, Reverend Claude A. Calcote, the then current pastor of Aveleigh Presbyterian, wrote about David Boozer's resting place:

*The lot have containing* [sic] *about one-eighth of an acre of ground is considered property of Aveleigh Church still. The high stone wall enclosing the tomb of Mr. and Mrs. David Boozer, the Garmany and Suber child, is the wall built with funds in Mr. David Boozer's will for this purpose back in the 19th century. The wooden cover has completely disappeared, along with many markers of other graves.*[24]

Sadly, Boozer's wishes eventually came to naught, as the Aveleigh Cemetery property was sold in the late twentieth century to a developer, who turned the site into a restaurant. Boozer's body now lies in Rosemont Cemetery in Newberry, South Carolina.[25]

In spite of O'Neall's claims, many in the Newberry community refused to accept financial setbacks as the cause of Boozer's death and blamed Amelia. She did not help matters by going to Columbia soon afterward to sell cotton. Amelia stayed there for two weeks before going to Charleston to meet an alleged lover. When she came back, she had a new carriage and wardrobe.[26]

The original site of David Boozer's grave. The Avaleigh Presbyterian Church sold the property to a national restaurant chain. *Photograph by the author.*

Consequently, Amelia was brought before Aveleigh Presbyterian on the charges that her "extravagance contributed" to Boozer's death. Listed among the extravagances were a "shawl, $60.00, silver forks and pearl handled knives." Furthermore she had received money for "1500 lbs. of cotton in Columbia and wasted the money." Additional charges included lying about receiving gifts and quarrelling with Boozer on the morning he killed himself.[27]

One of the more serious allegations was that Amelia was having inappropriate relationships with married men. One in particular was Dr. Hugh Huger Toland. Toland was born in Newberry County, South Carolina, in 1806 to an Irish immigrant who became a wealthy planter. A very intelligent child, he started school at four and won a reading prize at age six. At age sixteen, he apprenticed himself to a physician for eighteen months before entering the University of Transylvania in Kentucky, graduating first in his class in 1828. He later traveled to France for further study.[28]

Upon his return from France, Toland set up a practice in Newberry but, soon afterward, moved to Columbia, correctly thinking that his skills would be more appreciated there. In the late 1840s, he was making an annual income of $15,000 (about $455,000 today).[29]

Amelia agreed to the trial in the hope of ending gossip about her. The trial was heard before a moderator and several church members. (The church at the time had only twelve members.) Thanks to affidavits Amelia had collected and personal testimony from Dr. Toland, she was cleared of all charges.[30]

However, being cleared by her church did not mean that Amelia was innocent in the eyes of her neighbors. People started gossiping that Amelia was a "black widow" since three of her husbands had died while she was still so young. "Neighbors had been cool towards Amelia. Now she was held in contempt," wrote one person.[31]

The church hearing also tarnished Dr. Toland's reputation, as it made rumors of an affair between him and Amelia even stronger. He became so tired of the constant questioning about the affair that he lost his respect for his neighbors and moved to California, where he became a wealthy pioneering surgeon.[32]

Eventually, the members of Aveleigh Presbyterian expelled Amelia from the congregation for dressing unbecoming of a widow, her alleged affair and her "conduct in general."[33]

Amelia then moved from Newberry to Columbia, a decision she was pressured into making. There, Amelia met husband number four, Jacob Jefferson Norris Feaster, whom she married in 1852.[34]

Feaster, born in 1822 in Feasterville, South Carolina, was described as "a very worthy, clever man." At first, Feaster and his new family moved around, living in Alston and Greenville before settling for good in Columbia. By 1859, he and his brother, Trezvant D. Feaster, owned a grocery store at the corner of Richardson and Washington Streets in Columbia, about a block from the two-story house Jacob and Amelia lived in on the corner of Sumter and Washington Streets.[35]

Columbia was still a rather young town, having been founded in 1786 in order to move the state capital from Charleston to a more central location. By 1860, its population was 8,800, and the town was developing something of a cosmopolitan flair. It had two newspapers and several colleges and academies. During the legislative session, the city was filled with some of the richest and most powerful men in both South Carolina and the United States.[36]

The Feasters lived one block away from the Richland County Courthouse and Columbia's City Hall and four blocks from the South Carolina State

Site of the Feasters' house. The family lived here on the northwest corner of Sumter and Washington Streets. Their home was destroyed by fire on February 17, 1865. The Feaster store was where the second skyscraper from the left now stands. *Photograph by the author.*

House. This made their home the perfect place to be seen for someone desiring attention. Financially, they were very well off. Mr. Feaster owned $4,000 in real estate (about $114,000 today) and had a personal wealth of $30,000 (about $855,000 today).[37]

Amelia's fourth marriage went well at first, producing three children: Julia Carolina, born about 1854; Jacob Jr. ("Jack" or "Jakie"), born about 1856; and Ethland Brooks ("Tootie" or "Tutu"), born March 7, 1857, in Greenville. Marie would become especially close to Tootie. By all accounts, Marie and her new stepfather got along well and truly loved each other.[38]

In an undated poem, Amelia expressed her feelings of love toward her children, with Marie as the lily, Julia C. as the rose, Ethland as the violet and Jacob Jr. as the eagle.

> *Come list awhile my Daughters three,*
> *A Chaplet, I will weave for thee,*

# Early Life

*Of flowers pure, sweet and true*
*Colors, white, red and blue,*
*Lily, Rose and Violet.*
*My Lily's hair of auburn hue—*
*Her eyes of darkest deepest blue,*
*Displaying from her very birth*
*A Heart of warmth, a mind of worth,*
*Fair Child of promise now for Thee*
*I cull the flower of Purity.*
*Oh may thy pathway all through life*
*Be sweetly calm and free from strife,*
*Thy Mind to knowledge early given,*
*Thy Heart to Virtue and to Heaven,*
*This Lily is my prayer for Thee,*
*The eldest of my daughters three.*

*And now my little Rose for you*
*The weaving must begin anew,*
*My bright-eyed one for Thee I see*
*The greatest popularity*
*The favorite of the house and hall*
*The beauty of the garden wall,*
*Go forth and bloom in sweetest grace*
*Perfect in features, heart and face,*
*May Life glide sweetly on with Thee*
*Like sunbeams on a summer sea*
*Is Mother's prayer for Rosalie.*

*And now my little Violet blue,*
*What shall mamma say to you?*
*Gentlest, sweetest little flower*
*Unfolding new beauties every hour.*
*Oh may thy life be one bright dream*
*Untouched by sorrow, free from sin*
*Reward Thy Parent's tender care*
*With holy love and strive to be*
*Fit emblem of the name you bear,*
*Of charming little Modesty.*

*And now my boy, my Eagle Bird,*
*Such prophecy was never heard*
*As Mother would unfold for Thee*
*Thine eyes so full of sympathy*
*Proclaims Thy Soul's Nobility*
*Thy boyhood pure, thy manhood bright*
*Thine every act a Beacon bright*
*Thus shalt Thou be Thy Mother's joy*
*Thy Sisters' pride, Thy Pater's honest boy*
*Go forth and gain a noble name*
*Devote thy talents then to fame*
*Fear not be just! Thou then will be*
*Thy Country's Honor*
*And a Noble Son of Liberty.*[39]

Amelia and her family may have joined one of the two Episcopal churches in Columbia, Trinity or Christ Church, as Marie was later married in one and a granddaughter of Amelia would state that her family were Episcopalians. The Feaster home was almost halfway between the two congregations.

Sadly, the records for both churches were lost during the Civil War, so there is no way to tell if the Feasters were members of either congregation. Christ Episcopal was destroyed in the fire that ravaged Columbia on February 17, 1865, and though Trinity survived, its records were destroyed by Union soldiers. However, it would have been in keeping with Amelia's alleged social climbing ways if they were members of Trinity Episcopal Church, as two of Columbia's richest and most politically powerful families, the Hamptons and the Prestons, were members of that church.[40]

# CHAPTER 2
# The Civil War Years

Decades of sectional tensions came to a head on November 6, 1860, when Abraham Lincoln was elected president of the United States. A month later, on December 17, the State of South Carolina convened a Secession Convention at Columbia's First Baptist Church, less than a block from the Feasters' residence. After one day, the convention voted to adjourn to Charleston due to an alleged case of smallpox across the street from the church. On December 21, 1860, South Carolina formally seceded from the Union. On April 14, 1861, South Carolina troops fired at the Union garrison inside Fort Sumter in Charleston Harbor. The Civil War had begun.

Columbia would be one of the most loyal and patriotic cities in the Confederacy, but Amelia remained true to the Union. Though not surprising given her Philadelphia roots, Amelia's pro-Northern views made her stand out from most of her neighbors and, consequently, turned her into an outcast from Columbia's pro-Confederate society.

Margaret Narcissa Feaster, a niece of Jacob Sr., visited Columbia in August 1861. She spent a great deal of time with Marie and her mother. Young Margaret recorded the trip in her diary and wrote how the three ladies attended dress parades at the arsenal military school, and Margaret and Marie often went riding together.[41]

Sadly the happiness seems to have been short lived. Margaret Feaster makes no mention in her diary of a return trip to Columbia in March 1862, other than to say, "I have been to Columbia, did not enjoy my visit." Furthermore, she makes no further mention of her uncle Jacob or his family in her diary until 1865. By December 1864, it was gossiped that Amelia had left Mr. Feaster.[42]

However, it is possible that the Feasters' separation was due to Jacob Feaster's serving in the Confederate army. His obituary states he served in Colonel T.G. Tucker's last Regiment of Pioneers and the Highland Rifle Company, and James Williams states in his 1929 book, *Old and New Columbia*, that Jacob served in the army. However, the National Parks Service Civil War Soldiers and Sailors Database shows no record of Feaster serving in the Confederate army. On the other hand, there are two accounts that say Feaster ran a Confederate storehouse.[43]

One of Amelia's few remaining friends was Phineas F. Frazee, a Columbia coach maker originally from New Jersey who also held Unionist sentiments. Frazee lived on the corner of Assembly and Washington Streets, two blocks from the Feasters' home. Amelia may have been Frazee's only friend in Columbia, as the coach maker was whipped, tarred and feathered and run out of town because of his views.[44]

There were also allegations that Amelia was aiding and abetting Union spies, even going so far as to allow one to set up his base of operations in her home. Though she was never charged with anything, she was nonetheless kept under tight scrutiny.[45]

Then in the fall of 1864, a prisoners of war camp was set up in modern-day West Columbia to house captured Federal officers who were being sent from Charleston, many of whom had been relocated from Georgia because of Sherman's march through that state. An estimated 1,300 to 1,400 Federal officers were detained in a five-acre open field from October to December 1864. Though the camp was never given an official name, it was generally referred to as Camp Sorghum because sorghum molasses was the main food staple of the prisoners. The site was also known as Yankee City.[46]

It was not a very secure POW camp; 373 prisoners, almost one-third of the prison population, escaped due to the poor quality of the guards. Mary Chesnut wrote in November 1864 that "squads of Yankee prisoners escape every night." The guards were mostly raw recruits, often teenagers and elderly men, and despite the qualms about their "quality," under the circumstances, they were the only ones available. Often the prisoners would follow the Saluda River up to North Carolina, where Union sympathizers would guide them to the Federal lines in Tennessee.[47]

Amelia often visited and comforted the captured Federal officers held there. This continued after the prisoners were moved to the grounds of the

# The Civil War Years

In the fall of 1864, 1,300 to 1,400 captured Federal officers were held at Camp Sorghum in modern-day West Columbia, South Carolina. Amelia brought aid and comfort to many of them and helped some to escape. Today, the site is an unmarked vacant field. *Image courtesy of the South Carolina Confederate Relic Room and Military Museum, Columbia, South Carolina.*

State Asylum in the northeast part of Columbia in December 1864. Camp Asylum, nicknamed "Camp Lunacy" by the prisoners, was a more secure site as the prisoners were now surrounded by a brick wall. It also made them closer to her house.[48]

Amelia's interest in the prisoners is documented in this interesting letter in the *Official Records of the War of the Rebellion*, dated January 31, 1865:

> *I am instructed by General Winder to request that you grant permission to Captain McChesney, a prisoner of war now in your custody, to visit Mrs. Feaster at her residence near the market. The general has reliable information that this officer has on various occasions been very kind to our people. You will put him on his honor not to say or do anything against this country, and to return at such hours as you may designate (say 10 o'clock).*
>
> *Mrs. Feaster wishes him to come this evening.*[49]

A sketch of Camp Asylum. In the winter of 1864–65, the captured Federal officers were transferred from Camp Sorghum to this corner of the old South Carolina Mental Hospital complex. The prisoners nicknamed their new home "Camp Lunacy." *Image courtesy of the South Carolina Confederate Relic Room and Military Museum, Columbia, South Carolina.*

Site of Camp Asylum today. Despite the formidable obstacle this pre–Civil War brick wall presented, many prisoners were able to escape and find their way to the Feaster home. *Photograph by the author.*

According to Colonel James G. Gibbes, who was later mayor of Columbia, Amelia openly bragged that she "had done a great deal to assist Federal prisoners, and aided some to escape."[50]

One of those prisoners was Lieutenant Gilbert Sabre of the 2nd Rhode Island Cavalry, who had been held since December 1864 at Camp Asylum. He and several others POWs managed to hide for two days when Confederate officials evacuated the prison prior to Sherman's arrival. After being forced to leave their hiding place due to hunger and thirst, they ventured into Columbia. He later recalled:[51]

> *After entering the town, our first move was for the house of a lady whom we knew to be unquestionably of Union sentiments. We approached her door quietly. We knocked. The lady promptly responded. It was now several hours after midnight, and our sudden appearance at such a time somewhat agitated her.*
>
> *The door opened cautiously.*
> *"Who's there?" the lady whispered.*
> *"Friends," one of us replied.*
> *"Are you Union officers?" again she whispered, half in fear.*
> *"Yes," we replied.*
> *"Come in, then, quick," again she whispered.*
> *We went in, and related our story. The lady immediately gave us something to eat, and hid us away until the arrival of Sherman's army.*[52]

Sectional politics was not the only marital problem facing the Feasters. Virtually every Southern family experienced some financial hardship due to the war, thanks to the Confederacy's runaway inflation. In January 1862, $120 in Confederate notes bought $100 in gold. By January 1864, $1,800 in currency was worth $100 in gold. By December, it was $2,800. From then on, inflation raced even faster. It took $3,400 in currency to buy $100 in gold in January 1865 and $5,000 the next month.[53]

Consequently, the prices for food and other goods also went up. Corn rose from $25 a bushel in 1863 to $40 a bushel in January 1865. Bacon went from $1 a pound in 1863 to $5 a pound in 1864. In 1864, wood went for $34 a cord; by January 1865, it was $100. By 1864, flour went for $1,200 a barrel.

At the time, a common day laborer earned $10 a day, while a skilled one could earn $15. Confederate general Joseph Johnston, who moved to Columbia in the fall of 1864 to be near friends and family, found his $300 a month salary insufficient to make ends meet. In January 1865, he told a friend, "The expenses of living here [in Columbia] are much above our means. We can't remain [in Columbia] three months longer, even with Sherman's consent."[54]

The Feasters were not exempt from financial problems. But their problems may have been worse than those of some other Columbians because of Amelia's alleged free-spending ways. Colonel Gibbes recalled that the family was soon "in but modest circumstances, having lived very extravagantly."[55]

Marie, in the meantime, had become one of the most beautiful women in the state. As one writer waxed poetically:

> *She grew in grace and loveliness, and as she merged into womanhood, and became one of the most beautiful and fascinating young ladies in the whole state, and her personal charms were surpassed, if such was possible, by her brilliancy, her wit and charming manners. In fact she was said to be the perfect model of grace, beauty and loveliness. Her rare accomplishments and dazzling beauty, to say nothing of her wealth and social standing, made her without dispute the social queen of Columbia.*[56]

Marie was described as being of medium height with "golden hair, rose shades, blue orbs, healthy poised, delicious." Another wrote, "She was a beautiful blonde beyond description, rather small and always handsomely dressed." Edward Wells of the Charleston Light Dragoons remembered her as always being "dressed to kill" and compared her looks to those of Helen of Troy. One Columbian would recall that she had "wonderful blue eyes, bright curls and a complexion absolutely faultless."[57]

Famed diarist Mary Chesnut knew about Marie and may have known her personally. Chesnut agreed that Mary was "a beauty—that none can deny," while a friend of the diarist opined, "The girl's beauty is as plain as the nose on your face. It is so stupid to deny it." A student at South Carolina College (the present University of South Carolina) saw her "as possessed of the 'chic' and attractiveness of a Cleopatra." Another called her "the patron saint of the South Carolina College."[58]

Marie was perceived as being vain about her looks. "Boozer, who is always on exhibition—walking, riding, driving—wherever a woman's face can go, there is Boozer," wrote Mrs. Chesnut. Many writers commented that she drove around Columbia in an elegant equipage (a style of horse-drawn carriage) called the "Beauty Box." According to Robert de Treville Lawrence, it had a glass frame "well calculated to display the charms of its fair occupant" and "was always on the street when students were dismissed from class." Wells

# The Civil War Years

*Above*: Diarist Mary Chesnut and her husband, Brigadier General James Chesnut, rented this cottage in the fall and winter of 1864–65. From here, Mary noticed that Marie "was always on exhibition." *Photograph by the author.*

*Right*: Reportedly, Marie drove her carriage by South Carolina College, the modern-day University of South Carolina, everyday when the students got out of class. The all-male student body called her "the patron saint of the South Carolina College." *Photograph by the author.*

added, "Her dainty little feet rarely touch[ed] the pavement except when she was entering a shop." Lawrence's comments are backed by another local resident, who remembered that Marie "had one of the finest turnouts in the city, driving a pair of bob-tailed horses."[59]

She was also something of a "tom-boy" as she "enjoyed sliding down bannisters, playing with boys rather than girls and seemed perfectly independent and reckless in her movements—walking the streets with whom she pleased and at any hour." Despite this, "her beautiful face and figure, and sweet modest demeanor had secured for her, in spite of some protest from the grande dames of society, the entrée into circles in which her mother never could have appeared."[60]

Most accounts suggest that Marie was quite intelligent; she spoke fluent French and attended the best schools in Columbia at the time. One writer noted that Marie was known for her "brilliant though equivocal bon mots."[61]

We may never know where Marie went to school, but there are two strong candidates. The first is the South Carolina Female Collegiate Institute, commonly called the Barhamville Academy, located northeast of Columbia, near modern-day Two Notch Road. Founded in 1817 and named after Jane Barham Marks, the first wife of the school's founder, Dr. John E. Marks, the nonsectarian boarding school enjoyed an excellent national reputation for its academics and its faculty, which included many European-trained teachers. By 1850, it had over one hundred female students from all across the nation. Among its students were the daughter of Vice President John C. Calhoun and the mother of future president Theodore Roosevelt.[62]

Its academic year consisted of two terms, one from October to February and the other from February to June. In 1841, the school's tuition was $200 per school year, payable in advance, with classes in chemistry, botany, foreign languages, piano, music and embroidery costing extra, which could raise tuition to as much as $358.[63]

The other possible candidate would have been the Academy of the Immaculate Conception, a Catholic boarding school that was founded in 1852 and originally run by the Sisters of Mercy Order. They later turned the school over to nuns of the Ursuline Order, which, in turn, led to the school being commonly called "the Ursuline Convent." It was located at the corner of Main and Blanding Streets in a converted hotel, within easy walking distance of the Feaster house.[64]

The convent was also known for its academic excellence. "The ladies of the Ursuline Older are specially devoted to the education of young ladies. Their schools in Europe, as in the United States, have never failed to win and to retain the confidence of parents and guardians," said the school's promotional literature. The convent had two school terms, one from September to February, the second from February until July. In 1860, tuition for the Ursuline Covent for a boarding student was eighty dollars a term, payable in advance, and fifteen dollars for a day student. Music, Italian and French classes cost extra.[65]

Sadly, only a few of the pre–Civil War records of Barhamville survive, and Marie is not in any of them, while none of Ursuline Convent's records from that era still exist. It may never be known if Marie attended either one of the schools.

Despite her education, "some reported [Marie] as only a pretty doll, with no conversational powers," reported Lawrence. Another wrote that Marie had "a careless manner."[66]

Marie never lacked male suitors. Margaret Narcissa Feaster wrote that Marie often had male visitors come to her house at night. Another writer said that Marie's "hand was often sought in marriage by sons of the wealthy planters of upper tendom." One person recalled that the Feaster house "was nightly the resort of a crowd of young and old men fascinated beyond their judgment and wills." Among them was Confederate brigadier general Martin Gary, "who even dared to pay his attentions in public assemblies whereas others were shy of the questionable honor except in the privacy of [Marie's] home."[67]

By 1864, Marie was supposedly engaged to William "Willie" Henry Capers. Willie, born in 1844, was the son of Thomas F. Capers, a prominent Charleston planter. In December 1864, Confederate president Jefferson Davis sent a bill to the Confederate Senate asking that young Capers be assigned as aide-de-camp to Brigadier General Lucius Jeremiah Gartrell with the rank of first lieutenant.[68]

However, Willie's mother was not happy that her son was involved with the daughter of a known Union sympathizer and tried to discourage the marriage, although she had never heard anything bad about Marie herself. However, Mrs. Capers did not have to worry about a Yankee-in-law, as the engagement was broken off because, according to Mrs. Chesnut, Marie stole Willie's pocket watch and money.[69]

According to another account, it was Marie who would not marry Capers, and he was killed in battle a week after she turned down his proposal. However, the fact that Willie Capers survived the war, married Anna Margaret Missroon in 1869 and fathered six children severely tests the validity of this claim. The Capers lived for a while in New Jersey before moving to Mississippi, where Willie died in 1896.[70]

# THE SCANDALOUS LIVES OF CAROLINA BELLES MARIE BOOZER AND AMELIA FEASTER

General Preston and his son, William, may have hosted Marie as a guest in their home, the Hampton-Preston Mansion. The house is now a museum. *Photograph by the author.*

According to one biographer, Marie secretly loved Major William Preston, son of Brigadier General John S. Preston, superintendent of the Confederate Bureau of Conscription and a close personal friend of Confederate president Jefferson Davis. The Prestons were one of Columbia's leading and wealthiest families. General Preston himself had a high regard for Marie's looks, calling her "the most beautiful piece of flesh and blood [he] had ever beheld."[71]

It seemed that Marie would have made a good match, except for one small technical problem: it is not certain if William Preston knew of Marie's love for him or if he loved her. Some say Preston never suspected it and died at the Battle of Peachtree Creek outside Atlanta in July 1864 before Marie could tell him. Lawrence said that Marie claimed to have been engaged to a member of a "distinguished family" who was killed in battle. Years later, she named her son Preston, supposedly in honor of her first true love.[72]

For most of the war, Marie escaped some of the ostracizing her mother received, as she was thought of as a "good Rebel." Marie volunteered at the Wayside Hospital, often working side by side with relatives of William Preston. Mary Chesnut wrote in December 1864, "They say [Marie] is

Site of the Wayside Hospital. From 1862 until 1865, seventy-five thousand wounded soldiers received triage at this spot, where the South Carolina Railroad Deport stood. Marie's only know contribution to the war effort was to volunteer here as a nurse. *Photograph by the author.*

a good girl. Then why does she not marry some decent man, among the shoals who follow her, and be off, out of this tangle while she had a shred of reputation left?"[73]

But eventually Marie's Southern patriotism came into question. According to local gossip, "She was too vain and sensible of her attractiveness to allow a matter of patriotism to interfere with her ambition to attract admiration; so she soon numbered her victory from the ranks of men whom a short time before she had regarded as enemies." She was also criticized for not donating her horses to the Confederate military cause. Wells would caustically claim that "the 'dragoons' being properly behaved young men, of course would not have been acquainted with her."[74]

James Dunwoody Jones, a Confederate officer assigned to Camp Sorghum in the fall of 1864 recalled after the war:

> *A love affair came under my eye while I was at the Columbia prison camp…One of the inmates was a captain whose name I will withhold, as he was an estimable gentleman. In the North before the war he had met a woman [Marie], a great beauty of Columbia, South Carolina. When the fortunes of war brought him to that place as a prisoner, he renewed his*

# The Scandalous Lives of Carolina Belles Marie Boozer and Amelia Feaster

*friendship by mail…This friendly correspondence soon ripened the young man's feelings into love, and the couple became engaged.*[75]

According to Jones, Marie sent the captain a picture of herself, which Jones allowed the Union officer to keep, even though the camp's commandant had forbidden it. Later, this prisoner escaped and left with Sherman. Jones claimed that the two did get married, but there is no proof of this or, as we shall see, to another half dozen or so accounts of what happened to Marie.[76]

For most of the Civil War, South Carolina was spared the conflict's bloodshed with only the lower coastal region between Beaufort and Charleston seeing any significant action. That all changed in February 1865 when Major General William T. Sherman's sixty-thousand-plus-man juggernaut entered the state. On February 17, Sherman occupied Columbia, having met at best token opposition during his trek from Savannah, Georgia. Prior to Sherman's arrival, two of Marie's half siblings, Julia and Jakie, were sent from Columbia to Feasterville to be with relatives.[77]

That night, Columbia burned. Exactly when or who started the fire has been a major controversy for years. Regardless of its origins, the fire was fanned by high winds and raged until about four o'clock the next morning, destroying at least one-third of the city. Among the destroyed property was Jacob Feaster's store and residence.[78]

Lieutenant Sabre and his companions stayed with Amelia during Sherman's occupation of Columbia and tried to save her house. "Myself and [my] companions did all in our power to save her property, but without

After occupying Columbia on February 17, 1865, General William T. Sherman met Mrs. Feaster. He found Marie "beautiful." *Library of Congress.*

*Burning of Columbia.* This *Harper's Weekly Illustration* accurately captures the devastation of the fire that destroyed one-third of Columbia. The Feaster store is the large building in the foreground on the far left. *Author's collection.*

avail. The flames spread, and in the devouring element we saw the home of one who had been really a friend to us destroyed."[79]

This raises an interesting possibility. Amelia was on the "outs" with most people in Columbia, including her husband. Suddenly, she has a huge army sympathetic to her way of thinking occupying the city. Why not get back at her enemies by burning the town; something this army is already famous for? Perhaps it is possible that she found some soldiers to set the torch to her husband's store.

At first, this idea may seem far-fetched. However in his *Memoirs*, Sherman claimed the fire started near the county courthouse, which was across the street from Feaster's store. Regardless where the blaze began, several witnesses reported seeing Marie with many a bluecoat. Gibbes claimed that during the night, Amelia introduced herself to Sherman "as a Union woman." She then pointed to the Confederate warehouse, across the street from her burning residence, and told Sherman to have that fire put out since it was filled with bacon, flour, tobacco and cotton, which his army could use.[80]

However, the problem with this theory is that if there was any way Columbians could have linked the burning of their town to Amelia, they

When Sherman's army left Columbia, hundreds of refugees, consisting in part of Unionists and escaped slaves, accompanied the Federal army, including Amelia and Etland Feaster and Marie Boozer, in the "refugee train." *Author's collection.*

would have done so, and none of the contemporary accounts of the fire or Amelia's life make any such allegation.

On February 20, 1865, Sherman left Columbia. Marie, her mother and her sister Ethland joined several hundred refugees who accompanied the army. Many left to avoid poverty and starvation; others, like Amelia, left because of their pro-Northern views. According to Gibbes, Sherman, who found Marie "beautiful," gave the two horses that pulled their wagon to Amelia personally.[81]

Amelia's aid to the prisoners paid off for her. Lieutenant Sabre wrote, "It was now our turn to reciprocate the kindness extended to us. By permission of the provost-marshal the lady was allowed to accompany the army to Fayetteville, thence to Wilmington; and before leaving there, I had the satisfaction of seeing her comfortably situated with her relatives."[82]

Less than a month later, Mary Chesnut witnessed this conversation:

> "*Boozer went off with flying colors….She has married a Philadelphia officer.*"
> "*No doubt. And by this time she has married one from Boston—from New York—indiscriminately. Will she marry the Yankee army?*"[83]

Marie and her family made a very favorable impression on the troops. Soon, her family "traded up" for a fancy black carriage when some Union soldiers told a Mrs. Elmore that they needed the carriage for "a good Union lady." Mrs. Elmore responded by saying, "Then you do not want it for any one you will find here." To that a solider replied, "Oh! Yes; we've got two loyal ladies and we've got to have a carriage for them to go along with us." Marie and her mother got the carriage and supposedly $10,000 for destroyed cotton that neither Mrs. Feaster nor her daughters owned, though the person or persons responsible for these gifts were never identified.[84]

Sometime after that, a Mrs. Poppenheim was trying to see a Union general to arrange some protection when

> *the refugees from Columbia who followed Sherman's Army began to pass. Among them I recognized Mary Boozer and her mother in a carriage. She in a lovely conversation with a gay-looking officer riding in the carriage. The scene is so sickening I beg Mrs. Brown to let us go; waiting for the general won't pay.*[85]

A still popular tale alleges that Marie and Major General Judson Kilpatrick, Sherman's chief of cavalry, had an affair after she left Columbia, but this is nothing more than postwar fiction.[86]

According to another popular but fabricated story, Marie married a Lieutenant Wilson, but they separated in Wilmington, North Carolina, and never reunited. (Marie never went to Wilmington.)[87]

Once Marie Boozer crossed the North Carolina–South Carolina border, she probably never again set foot in the Palmetto State. In Fayetteville, North Carolina, she boarded the army tugboat *Davidson* and continued her journey up North.[88]

Robert de Treville Lawrence wrote that during the Federal occupation of Columbia, a "new-found friend" secured passage for Marie and her mother to go North. She was given a letter of introduction to be presented to a family she could stay with. Curiosity, however, got the best of her, and Marie opened the letter and discovered the introduction was for Marie to work as a maid for this family.[89]

Marie and her mother had not been doing all this social climbing for Marie to end up a maid. So according to Lawrence, when she arrived in Philadelphia, she posed as the daughter of an aristocratic Southern family. But the only part of this that is true is that Marie and Amelia did go to Philadelphia.[90]

## CHAPTER 3
# Up North

Amelia and her daughters arrived in Philadelphia sometime in late March 1865. Once there, they probably sought out relatives; Amelia's mother, Mary, was still alive. If so, this might have been the first time Marie and Ethland met their grandmother and other relatives. Why they left Philadelphia for New York is unknown, but given their short stay and that there is no mention of Amelia's side of the family in any known correspondence by Marie, it is probable that their visit did not go well.

While in Philadelphia, Amelia signed an affidavit on June 2, 1865, in defense of claims made by Phineas F. Frazee against the U.S. government for property lost in the burning of Columbia:

> Mrs. Amelia Feaster, being first duly sworn according to law, deposes and says: That she was born in said city of Philadelphia, and that she passed the period of her childhood in that city. That she has been well acquainted with Phineas F. Frazee, coachmaker, late of the city of Columbia in the State of South Carolina, and has been so acquainted for ten years last past. That she knows him to be a man of northern birth and education, and that his family reside in Rahway, New Jersey. Deponent was for a long time a resident of said city of Columbia, and her house in said city was on the same street with that of said Frazee, and distant one square therefrom. That she had frequent conversations with him before and since the commencement of the rebellion, and that she has always known him to be a strong friend of the Union, and knows that he was always so regarded

by the people of the said city of Columbia. Deponent knows that said Frazee was, while in said city, a constant and zealous friend of officers and soldiers of the United States held there as prisoners of war; that he supplied them freely with money, clothing, bedding, provisions, medicines, and various other necessaries and comforts, without any compensation or return other than their gratitude.

Deponent further says, that said Frazee, in consequence of his Union sentiments, which were well understood in said city of Columbia, and of his kindness as aforesaid to Union prisoners, was subjected to many insults and indignities of various descriptions, threatened with personal violence, and was actually thrown into prison. On one occasion, which was notorious in said city, he was severely whipped by a party that came to his house in the evening, sometime in 1863, and called him out for that purpose, and who shaved his head, and otherwise maltreated him.

Deponent further says, that said Frazee was generally known as a man of large property, the same being estimated at from two hundred to two hundred and fifty thousand dollars, and deponent having a general knowledge of said property, believes it to have been worth not less than two hundred thousand dollars in lawful money of the United States. She has also examined the schedule marked A, and attached to his memorial to the Secretary of War herewith, and must say that she believes it to contain a very moderate estimate of the value of the various items therein set down.

Deponent further says, that the United States forces, under Major General W.T. Sherman, entered said city of Columbia on the morning of the 17$^{th}$ of February, 1865, and in consequence of its occupancy by said forces, nearly the whole of it was destroyed by fire in the afternoon and evening of that day. That she was in the street watching the progress of the fire, and saw the property of said Frazee burned and totally destroyed.

Deponent further states, that she is, and ever has been a friend of the Union, anxious for its restoration, and hoping for the success of the Federal arms. She left the city of Columbia on the 20$^{th}$ of February, 1865, with the forces of General Sherman, and is now residing in said city of Philadelphia.[91]

When Amelia moved to New York City, she restated her assertion on December 16, 1865:

*Amelia Feaster, being duly sworn, deposes and says: That on the second day of June, 1865, she made an affidavit in the matter of the destruction of property of Mr. Phineas F. Frazee, late of the city of Columbia, South Carolina, on the night of the 17th of February last, and that the statement contained in the said affidavit she still affirms to be true.*

*Deponent further states, that the said city of Columbia was taken possession of by the United States forces about nine o'clock in the morning of the said 17th of February, and that no buildings were consumed by fire, except the Charlotte depot buildings, until after dark of said day; that said depot is full three-fourths of a mile from my house or said Frazee's, and did not contribute in any way [to] the destruction of said property of said Frazee; my house and out-buildings were set on fire by United States soldiers; I seen [sic] them do it, and I begged of them to desist, but they paid no attention to what I said; this was about ten o'clock in the evening, and when the engine was throwing water on the building the Federal soldiers would catch hold of the pipe and hose and throw the water away from the building; I then, with the help of Captain McChesney and Colonel Stevens, and other escaped prisoners, began to move my trunks and some things down the street, and stopped at the corner of Washington and Assembly streets, right by said Frazee's buildings; Mr. Frazee came to me and said, "You had better put your bed and trunks in my corner house"; a Federal soldier standing by, says, "H———ll! do you think them buildings won't be burnt? If you want to save your bed you had better keep it where it is; them buildings will burn before morning, and everything else in this city." I therefore did sit in the street, and I seen [sic] United States soldiers set fire to said Frazee's building, and watched the progress of the fire, and saw his dwelling houses, repository and offices of said Frazee's burned and totally destroyed by fire, occasioned by the said soldiers setting it on fire. A guard, holding Mr. Frazee's horse by the yard gate, was remonstrating with the soldiers, and told them that the horse and buildings was to be saved; that he was a special guard to take care of the horse; but they paid no attention; while they was [sic] talking others was sitting [sic] fire to the buildings, and he had to take the horse away.*

*Deponent further says, that she is and has been loyal to the United States Government, and left the city of Columbia with General Sherman's army on the twentieth day of February, 1865, with General Howard's headquarters', and now resides in the city of New York.*[92]

Frazee's petition was introduced in the U.S House of Representatives on January 12, 1866, and was referred to the House Committee on Claims. It was brought before the full House on February 2, 1866, where it was killed by a successful vote to table the measure.[93]

# The Scandalous Lives of Carolina Belles Marie Boozer and Amelia Feaster

Built in 1836, the Astor House was once one of the poshest hotels in New York City, hosting Abraham Lincoln en route to his first inauguration. However, by the 1870s, the Astor House started a decline that ultimately led to it being razed in 1926. *Library of Congress.*

Purportedly, Mrs. Feaster carried with her letters of introduction written by Sherman, Major General Oliver Otis Howard and Kilpatrick, with Sherman penning the lines that Amelia was "the only loyal lady he had met in South Carolina."[94]

Amelia and her daughters settled in the Astor House Hotel. An undated account from the *San Francisco Chronicle* claims that they were assisted financially by the Union League Club of New York, a wealthy, conservative group founded to aid the Northern war cause in 1863. However, there is nothing in the 1879 history of the club that makes mention of giving assistance to exiled Unionists or anyone else during this time, nor is there anything in the club's records showing that it gave the ladies any financial assistance. There were also claims that the New York newspapers made appeals on behalf of the women, generating thousands of dollars, but there is no hard evidence of that either.[95]

However, novelist/historian Elizabeth Boatwright Coker claimed in a 1959 speech that the Union League destroyed all its records but "the secretary of the club during those years was the grandfather of a friend—and he had his grandfather's original notes of the proceedings!"[96]

# Up North

Columbia mayor James Gibbes met Amelia in December 1865 and had to decline her request to declare her still-living husband dead. *Author's collection.*

According to Mrs. Coker's version of the story in her novel *La Belle*, Amelia was given $10,000 by the Union League, and it was all gone in eight months. In addition, the organization paid the Astor House $2,000 for the ladies' boarding to prevent Amelia and her daughters from being evicted.[97]

While in New York, Ethland was educated at the Convent of the Sacred Heart for six years.[98]

Apparently Frazee's petition inspired Amelia to file one of her own. During a business trip to New York in December 1865, Colonel Gibbes responded to Amelia's request for a visit. Gibbes found Amelia "living in style, with a handsome suite of rooms and surrounded by a number of army officers." Gibbes quickly learned why she asked him to stop by: "She was they're [sic] working up her claim for loyalty and wanted me to give her a certificate as Mayor of Columbia that she was a widow." Gibbes could not help her, as he had seen her still living husband, Jacob Feaster, only a few days earlier.[99]

Gibbes's visit brings up an interesting question: What was Jacob and Amelia's marital status? Clearly, the two had been separated prior to Amelia's leaving Columbia, but were they ever divorced? Circumstantial evidence suggests that they never were.

Amelia's request of Colonel Gibbes implies that she and Jacob were still legally married in late 1865, which coincides with all contemporary accounts that the Feasters were only separated or living apart. Also, Jacob did not remarry while Amelia was still alive, even though Amelia tried to pass herself off as a widow. Furthermore, there is no known record of a

45

divorce, though any such record prior to 1865 could have been destroyed during the burning of Columbia.[100]

Coker, in *La Belle*, states that Colonel Gibbes intervened on Amelia's behalf and convinced the Astor House's manager to let Amelia and her children stay one more month, provided that they married into money and settled their debts at that time.[101]

Despite the setback, Amelia pressed on, and on June 26, 1866, U.S. senator John Sherman, the brother of General Sherman, "presented

One of the most powerful and influential lawmakers of the late nineteenth century, Senator John Sherman, the general's brother, introduced a bill to award Amelia $10,000. *Library of Congress.*

the memorial of Amelia Feaster, praying to be reimbursed for moneys expended in alleviating the condition of Union officers confined in the rebel prison at Columbia, South Carolina; which was referred to the Committee on Claims."[102]

That Sherman, known for being a reform-minded fiscal conservative, introduced the measure is a bit odd, unless he did it on his brother's behalf. This is possible since the two men were quite close. However, there is no known correspondence between the two mentioning Mrs. Feaster. Nor is there any evidence that the two men saw each other in person after the Grand Review of the Union armies in May 1865 until the autumn of 1866.[103]

On July 5, Senator Sherman tried to have the bill moved from the U.S. Senate's Committee on Claims to the Committee on Military Affairs and the Militia, but the Senate voted it down. The Committee on Claims reported the matter to the full Senate on July 16 as Senate Bill Number 434, *A Bill for the Relief of Mrs. Amelia Feaster, of Columbia, South Carolina*, which read:

> *Be it enacted by the Senate and House of Representatives of the United States of America in Congress assembled, that the Secretary of the Treasury, be and is hereby authorized and required to pay to Mrs. Amelia Feaster, of Columbia, S.C. out of any money in the Treasury not otherwise appropriated, the sum of ten thousand dollars as a reimbursement for money expended by her in alleviating the suffering of the officer and soldiers of the United States army, confined in the rebel prisons in that city during the late rebellion.*[104]

The $10,000 appropriation would equal about $149,000 today. Accompanying the bill were the "petition and papers relative to the claim of Mrs. Amelia Feaster."[105]

In her petition, Amelia "claims that she is and ever has been a loyal citizen of the United States, formerly resident in Philadelphia, Pennsylvania, but during the rebellion residing in the city of Columbia, South Carolina, till the 20th of February, 1865, when she left that city and came north with General Sherman's army.[106]

Amelia further asserted that she was an angel of mercy to the Union prisoners held at Camp Sorghum and confirmed the allegations that she aided and abetted escapes from the camp:

> *Between October 1, 1864, and February 14, 1865, 1,200 Union officers were prisoners of war at Columbia, South Carolina. It appears from the*

*evidence that Mrs. Feaster was then a wealthy widow lady of that city, and devoted to the Union cause. Being applied to by the Union officers in the prisons for books, etc., she immediately supplied every one whom she could reach, and not only supplied them with books, but also very liberally with clothing, blankets, provisions, medicines, and money; she also gave great quantities of such things, and meat daily to the sick inmates of hospitals, who had none supplied to them by the rebel authorities; she also gave the necessary information to facilitate the escape of prisoners, concealing them in her own house, and furnishing them with money, maps of the country, and guides to prosecute their escape. For all these acts she suffered suspicion and contumely, and on two occasions was arrested by the rebel authorities, her life was threatened, and she was forbidden to pass to the place where our men were confined; notwithstanding which she continued her labors, often accomplishing the desired end by bribing the guards with money, until Sherman's army entered the city.*[107]

Two things stand out about the petition. First is that Amelia Feaster is incorrectly referred to as a "widow," meaning she was still trying to pass herself off as one and therefore guilty of perjury. The second is her claim that she was arrested twice by Confederate authorities. There is no mention of her ever being arrested in any other account of her life, even the most slanderous ones. However, it is quite possible that she was questioned by local officials about her doings, which she decided to spin as an arrest in order to help her case.

The petition continues, "These things are stated and sworn to by very many prisoners, the names of some of whom are given below, and whose statements and letters have been examined by the committee. Some of these papers are addressed to the President, the Secretary of War, and the Secretary of the Interior, and to members of Congress."[108]

Attached to the petition were the names of two dozen U.S. Army and Navy officers of all ranks from seven states and two endorsements from eyewitnesses.[109]

The first endorsement came from Captain Emlen N. Carpenter of the 6th Pennsylvania Cavalry. The captain wrote:

*Fayetteville, N.C, March 12, 1865.*

*I certify, &C, I was captured by the enemy at the battle of Todd's Tavern, a cavalry engagement, immediately preceding that of Spotsylvania Court*

# Up North

*House, Virginia, on the 7th of May, 1864, and was held as a prisoner of war until the 17th day of February, 1865, when I escaped. The condition of the officers (prisoners of war) was pitiable; without sufficient clothing or food, and deprived of many of the necessaries of life.*

*Shortly after we were moved to Columbia, Mrs. Feaster, a lady of Philadelphia, whose sentiments are those of the supporters of the government of the United States, interested herself in my behalf—daring the laws prohibiting [it]. She furnished me, and through me several other officers, with food and clothing; kept me informed of the movements of General Sherman's army, as far as was known in the city, so that I was enabled to make every preparation and effect my escape. I went to her house in Columbia three days preceding the entree [sic] of General Sherman into the city, and was concealed there—the city, at that time, being filled with rebel troops.*

*Mrs. Feaster was subjected to continual annoyance and suspicion on account of her too evident sympathy with the Union cause, and her endeavors to alleviate the sufferings of the prisoners of war.*

*During the conflagration of Columbia her dwelling and storehouses, together with a large amount of valuable property, were destroyed.*

*Under the protection of Major General Howard she has accompanied the army to this place.*[110]

The second endorsement came from Edward E. Kendrick Jr., the former adjutant of the 10th New Jersey Veteran Volunteers. He wrote:

*New York, June 12, 1865.*

*SIR: I beg that you will allow me the pleasure and duty of gratitude which I owe to Mrs. Amelia Feaster and daughter, Miss Maria [sic] Boozier, late of Columbia, South Carolina, to speak of their self-sacrificing attentions to the Union officers confined for several months in prison at Columbia, of whom I was one, furnishing food, shelter, raiment, and money to release us from starvation and suffering. While we were deprived of animal food for five months, without shelter, with dilapidated clothing, shoeless and hatless, suffering, sick and dying, they, with their money, though not allowed inside of the ground of the stockade, would place the means in the hands of the confederate sutler to buy food and clothing to be handed to us.*

*To the sick in the prison hospital substantial food and delicacies were received indefinitely from their hands, they not being allowed themselves to* aid us under severe punishment, during the winter of 1864–'65; while we were suffering from cold and wet, they sent us, in their own wagons, liberal supplies of wood to keep us warm, and (by remuneration) the guard passed it through the lines as from the confederate government, otherwise it would have been stopped and they arrested.

In addition to depositing money in the hands of the confederate sutler, they paid sums of money, bribing the guard of the prison to distribute money, and sometimes to gain access to us in the prison yard of the jail; and they have also been the means of aiding us to escape, which I did in November last, but was recaptured and returned in three weeks. Their house was an asylum and retreat if we escaped, where we were concealed until arrangements were made for guides, &c, to carry us away. The confederate authorities were very suspicious of them; but so discreet and secretly did they manage, no positive charge of aiding us could be made against them. Their money, lavished upon the guard and officer having us in keeping, kept the secret from publicity. When General Sherman entered Columbia, (I was removed the day previous,) they had concealed in their dwelling several Union officers.[111]

The committee report adds, "Major General Sherman also states that Mrs. Feaster's property in Columbia was destroyed by fire, so that she is now reduced to poverty and want."[112]

The committee concluded:

In her memorial, Mrs. Feaster claims to have incurred an outlay of sixty thousand dollars in her benefactions for our officers in prison. General Howard says in his endorsement of Mrs. Feaster's memorial: "The government of the United States cannot do too much for those kind friends to our prisoners who were in that sad extremity. I have no knowledge of the loss sustained, but would be glad if some relief could be granted."

General Terry concurs in the above endorsement of General Howard. Under the usages of the government, and as it is prohibited by existing law, Mrs. Feaster cannot receive any compensation for the property lost through the casualties of war, but she ought, in common justice, and in view of her self-sacrificing devotion to the Union cause, for which she expended so freely her ample means without expecting any return therefore, by which she contributed so much to the necessities of the needy and distressed prisoners, to be remunerated in part for the money so nobly expended.

The committee having carefully considered the allegations and proofs in this case, and the recommendations of Generals Grant, Howard, Terry,

> *Kilpatrick, and Ed. Schriver, consider that the case is a meritorious one; and, in view of the undoubted fact that, through the misfortunes of war, the petitioner is now rendered houseless, homeless, and moneyless, report the accompany bill, and recommend its passage.*[113]

The Senate passed bill 434 by unanimous consent on July 17, 1866. The bill was sent to the U.S. House of Representatives the next day and was referred to the House Committee on Claims on July 24, where it remained until December 18, 1866, when the bill was tabled by the full House on a motion by Republican congressman William B. Washburn of Massachusetts, effectively killing the petition.[114]

Since motions to table are not debatable, there is no record of why the House voted as it did. Because several similar petitions were treated in a like manner that same day, Amelia's defeat could have been nothing more than a reflection of the mood of Congress.

The man who made the motion, Representative Washburn, was a reform-minded conservative banker who served on the House Committee on Claims for ten years and was at one time its chairman. According to the *Biographical Encyclopedia of Massachusetts of the Nineteenth Century, Volume 2*, during Congressman Washburn's tenure on the committee, three to four thousand cases were heard and none of the recommendations of the committee were ever overruled by the full House.[115]

On the other hand, the bill could have died because Amelia's notorious past had finally caught up with her and there were accusations that she was trying to profit off the prisoners. In an undated letter, Captain Carpenter, who had provided the first affidavit supporting Amelia's petition, turned on her, accusing Amelia in a letter that "your system of aiding prisoners of war is a deep laid scheme for converting Confederate money into good money."[116]

The captain took umbrage at her claims that she spent half a million dollars helping POWs escape and that she gave him and his brother $100,000 in gold prior to Sherman's arrival in Columbia in February 1865. "This is too ridiculous to need a comment," wrote Carpenter. He further accused her of telling people in Philadelphia that she had lent the captain $2,500 to $5,000. "Of course I have contradicted the report and denied the possibility of you having made such statements." The captain threatened to report her to the War Department, unless she would "place in my hands a written retraction, contradiction or whatever you choose to call it."[117]

Despite Amelia's lack of success in Congress, rumors would fly for years that she received money from Washington. The amounts she got would vary from gossip to gossip. One claimed she received the $10,000 she asked for, while another said it was $15,000. Another writer said Amelia received $30,000 from Congress, while one person made the incredible claim that Amelia received $10 million.[118]

In the meantime, Marie met and married John S. Beecher, a New York City importer who was "many years [Marie's] senior." Exactly when Beecher was born is a mystery, as he does not appear in any census records, though assuming that he was in his twenties when he went into business in the 1850s, it is probable that he was born in the 1830s or late 1820s, making him ten to twenty years older than Marie.[119]

In *La Belle*, Mrs. Coker describes Beecher as being a member of an "excellent New England" family who was in his early forties with "a long head and a pointed nose and…blond [hair] mixed with gray," which he kept long. He also had long sideburns and a mustache and green eyes. Sadly, we do not know if this description came from Coker's research or her imagination. Adding to the mystery is that there was a prominent New York farmer with the same name who is often misidentified as Marie's husband.[120]

Beecher had gone in business in 1855 with Fredrick E. Ives and founded the firm Ives, Beecher & Co., which the *New York Times* described in 1894 as "one of the most extensive importing and mercantile establishments in the country."[121]

At this time, Beecher was also a member of the Exempt Engine Company, a reserve fire brigade. This group later became a part of the 11th New York Infantry, a Zouaves unit in the Civil War, but there is no record of Beecher serving with this unit.[122]

In 1863, he and his partners moved their business to 98 Front Street in Manhattan, where they imported whiskey, wines and tea. The 1876 New York City Directory lists his home as a farm in New Jersey. An 1884 report shows that his New York property covered nine acres and his New Jersey farm 190.[123]

Marie and Beecher were married in either December 1865 or January 1866, possibly in an Episcopal Church. According to Mrs. Coker in *La Belle*, Amelia forced Marie into the marriage in order to be rich again and because the Astor House was suing Amelia for indebtedness. She also supposedly moved in with the newlyweds.[124]

One popular legend says that Beecher gave his wife $150,000 as a wedding gift. The newlyweds honeymooned in Europe and, upon their return to New York, moved into a house on Sixteenth Street near Fifth Avenue. They summered at Newport and had a box at the opera. Marie also had a pony and a carriage at her beck and call.[125]

Marie's marriage to Beecher produced a son, John Preston Beecher, who was born on January 6, 1867. However, it was not a happy marriage. Marie found Beecher to be very controlling. She grew tired of him and soon had her sights on another man, Lloyd Phoenix.[126]

Phoenix was a member of a distinguished New York family. He was born in 1841 and was an 1861 graduate of the U.S. Naval Academy. He served in the U.S. Navy throughout the Civil War. Phoenix resigned his commission as a lieutenant when the war ended, becoming an avid yachtsman and a member of several prominent New York City clubs.[127]

Exactly how "close" Marie was to Phoenix is uncertain, but their relationship was certainly the subject of gossip. Regardless of how close they were, it was too close for Beecher, who divorced Marie by 1868.[128]

The divorce was disastrous for Marie. She later wrote, "I was cheated out of my home and property by J.S.B. who made me sign a paper—on condition of having Preston with me. But afterwards he kept Preston and the property too." Marie's comment suggests that Beecher may have been unfaithful himself. In fact, Wells wrote that Beecher "was by profession a philanthropist, in practice a philogynist [womanizer]." Marie's flirtations with Phoenix were all for naught, as he apparently never had any interest in marrying anyone. He died a bachelor in 1926.[129]

In fairness to Beecher, he did provide Preston with a good education. Marie's only child graduated from St. Paul's School, a New Hampshire Episcopal boarding school, in 1885. Preston went on to Columbia College (now University) in New York and studied medicine. He was also educated in London and Paris.[130]

In the long run, the collapse of Marie's marriage to Beecher was a good thing for her. In 1884, Ives, Beecher & Co. found itself in bankruptcy with $556,291.69 in liabilities, with Beecher personally owing creditors $81,244.45. Beecher blamed his firm's woes on the failure of Congress to pass a whiskey bill, which led to a depressed whiskey market, and his own poor health. While the divorce saved Marie from Beecher's financial catastrophe, their separation, more importantly, allowed her to find the man she would find true happiness with.[131]

After her failed attempt to obtain money from Congress, Amelia all but disappeared from history. Eventually, Julia and Jacob Jr. joined Amelia in New York City, where she died on November 2, 1870, from dropsy, a nineteenth-century term for edema, a medical condition that causes swelling of limbs and organs and is often caused by illness or injury. She was buried in Philadelphia. According to biographer Julian Selby, she was broke at the time of her death and had been befriended by a Mr. Bostwick, who had once lived in Columbia.[132]

Meanwhile, the man she tried to declare dead, Jacob Feaster, outlived Amelia by twenty-five years. He moved to LaGrange, Florida, in 1867 with two brothers, a sister and an uncle and spent the rest of his life there. He was eventually joined by his three children from his marriage to Amelia, though Jacob Jr. died sometime after 1870. The elder Feaster remarried in 1874 to Jeanette E. Twichell, with whom he had four more children. He died on January 18, 1895, from complications from overheating.[133]

Circumstantial evidence, based on the few known letters written by Marie and her relatives, suggests that she continued to enjoy a friendly relationship after the Civil War with her stepfather and half siblings. It is questionable, though, if she ever saw Jacob Feaster or any of her half siblings, save Ethland, after her divorce from Beecher.

CHAPTER 4

# The Countess de Pourtalès

The exact whereabouts of Marie immediately following her divorce are unclear. She was living in Paris by 1870, where she presented herself as Miss Marie Beauvar Boosier of New Orleans so no one in Columbia or New York could tattle on her. Eventually, her sister Ethland joined her in 1871 or 1872 and attended a French Catholic school before returning to America in 1874. Marie may have returned with Ethland, as she was in Baltimore by the mid-1870s.[134]

In Baltimore, Marie met and became engaged to French nobleman Count Arthur de Pourtalès-Gorgier. Born in 1844 in the Gorgier-Neuchâtel region along the French-Swiss border, the count was a member of a large and ancient family of German, French and Swiss nobility who were active in foreign services. In 1904, the New York *Globe and Commercial Advertiser* wrote, "It has been said of the Pourtales families of Germany and France that more American women have married into it than any other prominent European house."[135]

The count's mother, Anne, was the Countess of Escherny, while a grandfather had been a chamberlain at the Prussian court. Arthur de Pourtalès was a career diplomat serving as secretary to the French Legation in Washington, D.C.[136]

The count was a widower. His first marriage was to Jennie Lind Holladay (1851–1873), the daughter of Benjamin "Ben" Holladay. Holladay's creation of an overland stagecoach route during the California gold rush led to his being called the "Stagecoach King."[137]

# The Scandalous Lives of Carolina Belles Marie Boozer and Amelia Feaster

This rare image of Marie Boozer was made after her first marriage and is the last known image of her. Sadly, there are no known images of her two husbands. *Author's collection.*

Arthur and Jennie were joined together in an elaborate wedding in 1869 at the count's family's French château. Two years later, they welcomed a daughter named either Jenny or Bertha. However, Count de Pourtalès's first marriage was short-lived, as Jennie died in 1873. How she died is a bit of a mystery. One account stated she died "in a rather tragic manner" on a train "just as it entered [the] bridge at Aurora, Ill. from an overdose of morphine," which some say was deliberate. But another stated that Jennie suffered from a "congestive chill," which was a nineteenth-century term for malaria-like symptoms accompanied by diarrhea. However, an account in the August 27, 1898 edition of the *Chicago Tribune* said the accident took place between Philadelphia and Washington.[138]

Prior to their marriage, Arthur and Marie came to New York. They stayed at the Metropolitan Hotel with the supposed intent to visit Washington and then Florida for the winter, possibly to visit Marie's family. Apparently a mistake was made, and Marie was listed as the count's first wife, Jenny. It was eventually retracted, but Marie's identity was not shared.[139]

Reportedly, Holladay was not happy about any of this. The *San Francisco Chronicle* on January 6, 1876, wrote a full "exposé" on the situation that may or may not be taken with a grain of salt:

> *The great sorrow of the millionaire's heart is that his son-in-law, the Count Arthur De Pourtales, has lately given the little girl a stepmother, and that stepmother is Mrs. John S. Beecher, whose career in New York and London, Paris, Nice and other cities of Europe is well known to the readers of the London* Daily News, *and the inhabitants of those cities.*[140]

## The Countess de Pourtalès

According to the story, Holladay had arranged for the count to receive $500 a month for the care and well-being of his granddaughter and had planned on continuing the stipend, even if the count remarried. But apparently, the count's making Marie the new stepmother for Holladay's granddaughter was too much for the "Stagecoach King." When Holladay's business agent, George K. Otis, visited the count, Arthur denied being married to Marie at first, telling Otis that she was Mrs. Beecher and that she had been kind to his baby. Otis in turn remarked that Marie's name had been linked to several London scandals and said that if he were in the count's shoes, he "would take a pistol and blow my brains out."[141]

Arthur did not follow that gruesome advice but did await the arrival of the Holladays for a prearranged meeting. Holladay by now had no desire to see his former son-in-law or his family but agreed to give the count $1,000 if he allowed the Holladays to adopt their granddaughter. The count and Mr. Holladay met at the Hotel Brunswick, but after reading the terms of the agreement, Arthur refused to sign the paperwork.[142]

The newspaper account ends coldly:

> *Now this little girl passes from Mr. Holladay's hands into that of a father in whom he can have no confidence. Who has deceived the trust that he reposed in him, and into the care and supervision of a woman that Mr. Holladay can never receive into his family, and that he regards as totally unfit and unworthy to be the guide and guardian of any child.*[143]

An "eyewitness" account of Marie's second wedding that appeared in the March 16, 1894 edition of the *(Atlanta, GA) Constitution* relates a similar tale. Reportedly when Holladay was informed, at the time of the wedding, of the true identity of his granddaughter's new stepmother, "his rage knew no bounds, as well as his indignation." The account also says that Holladay cut off financial support to his former son-in-law. There may some truth to these tales, as there is no mention of Jenny's grandparents in the few known letters written by Marie.[144]

Despite this setback, Marie and Arthur were married on May 2, 1876, in Baltimore, Maryland. Baltimore is the oldest and premier Catholic diocese, with the Archbishop of Baltimore still enjoying today the right of precedence above all other bishops and archbishops in the United States, which is perhaps why the Catholic diplomat was married there. Their wedding may have been performed by Archbishop James Roosevelt Bayley.[145]

They honeymooned in Shanghai and Hong Kong, where they were fêted for four days by Governor Pope Hennessey before returning to France on

## The Scandalous Lives of Carolina Belles Marie Boozer and Amelia Feaster

January 13, 1878. Upon her arrival in Marseilles, Marie wrote to Ethland, "I cannot begin to describe to you how interesting the voyage has been."[146]

Marie went on to discuss what she had seen and experienced in the East, calling Shanghai "a perfect European City, beautiful houses, horse, carriages and good society." Marie called Hong Kong "a perfectly lovely spot...one of the prettiest little places imaginable." She was particularly taken with the governor's palace in Hong Kong, calling it "a perfect palace of a home...such splendor as [the governor] lives in is beyond description!"[147]

Upon their return to Europe, the de Pourtalèses went to Naples, where they visited the Pompeii museum, which Marie found "intensely interesting," though of the city as a whole she said, "Naples is a pretty place but less so than Florence or Rome naturally."[148]

Marie's second marriage was a happy one. She told a relative, "Yes I am in good health and am perfectly happy in my husband's love and devotion, and I adore him. He is a charming, refined, and distinguished man, and very handsome and above all, he is good, and has every noble trait, and a heart of gold." The only problem in their marriage was that the "pay has not been that great."[149]

In an 1884 letter to her sister Tutu, Marie wrote, "I am heart, body and soul devoted to my husband and my life very calm, very happy and very perfect, I regret nothing. I am too happy in my present to even recall the past."[150]

One of Arthur's first post-marriage postings was Japan, where he and Marie resided for five years. One account says that the count begged for this posting to get away from Holladay, but it cannot be confirmed nor seems likely.[151]

It was during this period that something unfortunate may have happened, for there were numerous published accounts about Marie having misadventures in Japan. Marie herself alluded to this when she wrote about her time in Tokyo: "I loved it and regret it." The *Washington Post* in 1905 noted that Marie was gossiped about in Japan, which raises the question what happened.[152]

A fake "obituary" published in the *Augusta (GA) Chronicle* on September 18, 1927, and later reprinted at face value in *The Women of the Confederacy*, stated, "[Marie's] charms ensnare[d] a number of important officials in the Mikado's [emperor's] government. Divorced by the French ambassador, she married the Japanese Prime Minister, who finally wearying of her continued indiscretions, had her thrown into prison and beheaded." The *Chicago Tribune* wrote in 1898 that such stories about Marie in Japan were "fairy tales...for they are nothing else." It also noted that the gossip had annoyed and disgusted the count.[153]

## The Countess de Pourtalès

Since the evidence is clear that Marie's second marriage was happy and she was a loving wife, totally devoted and faithful to her husband, it seems unlikely that Marie would have had an affair. Perhaps she got too friendly or flirtatious with someone, and their relationship was misinterpreted. Or possibly another Countess de Pourtalès did something scandalous and Marie got the blame. We might never know.

After the Japanese posting, the de Pourtalèses went to Guatemala for three years and then spent two years in Italy. By 1883, they were assigned to the Dutch West Indies, modern-day Indonesia, living in Buitenzorg on the island of Java. Though the coastal city of Batavia (modern-day Jakarta) was the official capital of the colony, Buitenzorg (modern-day Bogor) was the de facto capital of the colony. Built on the hills along the Salak Volcano about sixty kilometers south of Batavia, it started out as the eighteenth-century summer home of a Dutch official, but in 1808, the colony's governor general decided to move his home and many administrative offices to Buitenzorg. By the time the de Pourtalèses arrived, it was an exclusive European-style community whose population consisted mainly of rich and powerful white people, with nonwhites (mostly servants) only being allowed to live in designated neighborhoods. The town was noted for its many well-manicured gardens.[154]

Their life there was bucolic. Marie described Buitenzorg as "one of the prettiest [places] I have ever seen. Every house is a villa surrounded with marble floors, fine large rooms and comfortable." Their home was "perfectly situated" with a view that was "lovely" with nearby mountains. She described the weather as "a perpetual spring with cool nights...the air is pure, cool and sweet." Her husband was "an intimate and chosen friend" of the governor general.[155]

However, Marie also found it "a dull little place." "Our amusements are not many," she wrote. "Once a week dinner at the palace and now and then card parties. The good people of the palace are usually well educated but are totally wanting in usage de monde—they have no idea of 'receiving.'"[156]

Jenny was with her father and stepmother during the count's posting in Java. Marie lovingly called her "my little girl" and hired an educated governess for her. "I need have no care for my daughter. Her education is as thorough here as in Europe. I adore her and she worships me. I never knew such devotion. She is so clever, so refined, so well brought up, such a little lady. I am repaid a thousand times in her. She is quite like my own child."[157]

Despite her new life as a world traveler, Marie never forgot her son, Preston. She told her sister, "I don't care if Preston loves me or not. His

*Krakatoa.* This illustration shows the eruption of August 26–27, 1883. When the volcano blew up, it created the loudest recorded explosion in human history. Though the de Pourtles were less than one hundred miles away from the eruption, their location on the island of Java prevented them from being one of the over thirty-six thousand known casualties from the event. *Library of Congress.*

father always swears he does not teach him to forget me, but he is a liar. It is natural for a child to forget when separated for years but I don't take it to heart." She added, "If I could see him, I should be pleased, but I love my little daughter too well to have any room for any heartaches.[158]

On August 26, 1883, the de Pourtalèses found themselves less than one hundred miles from the island of Krakatoa when it had the loudest volcanic eruption in recorded history. In the wake of the explosion, 165 villages were destroyed, 36,417 people were killed and untold thousands were injured. Most of the casualties did not come from the eruption directly (the island was deserted) but from ensuing tsunamis.[159]

In addition, the eruption sent ash and rock as high as 120,000 feet, if not higher, and it remained there for five years. As a result, sunrises and sunsets around the planet were more colorful and vivid. However, a far more serious threat was that the Earth dropped a full degree Fahrenheit in temperature due to the ash in the atmosphere. In the wake of the explosions, the island of Krakatoa disappeared into the sea.[160]

In the capital city of Batavia, eighty-three miles away, "a wall of water" rushed into the city's canal system, causing the water level to rise by several feet and causing hundreds of merchants and residents along its banks to flee for safety two and half hours after the massive explosion. Later that day, a far worse wave, at least seven and half feet in height, came in and then fell back ten feet below sea level. This pattern would be repeated fourteen times over the next twenty-eight and half hours, with the wave extremes lessening each time before things went back to normal.

Thanks to the geography of Java and Buitenzorg's location on the island, the de Pourtalèses were spared the worse of the explosion. Marie told Ethland that tales of the disaster were "much exaggerated" though "to me it was bad and horrible enough, but we escaped everything!" She wrote, "Of course there was the fearful noise like the firing of many and great cannons at intervals of every 8 minutes. Then the sky was obscured by a thick yellowish cloud and one could hear the falling of something like very fine soft rain. And by and by one perceived the ground and leaves covered with grey dust which proved to be the rain of ashes."[161]

According to Marie, "The only effect felt here and at Batavia was the noise and vibration but I assure you although I was not at all alarmed it was not 'gay.' Thousands of people were destroyed, but they were Chinese and Malays—only about 10 Europeans—fortunately. The sea swept over the town with tremendous force and receded carrying all with it into the main ocean. It was terrible!"[162]

Arthur's posting to Java ended soon after the natural disaster. By 1885, he and Marie were living in Switzerland.[163]

On March 25, 1895, the Pourtalèses arrived in New York aboard the *La Champagne.* This was probably Marie's last visit to America. The exact purpose is unclear, but it may have been a diplomatic mission for the count.

Sometime after their return to France, Count de Pourtalès came close to losing a second wife to a train accident. After taking the *Bretagne* from New York back to France, Marie took the boat's special train for Paris. Just before reaching Rouen, while the train was in a long tunnel, she mistook the carriage door for that of the toilet room and was "pitched" out of the train. She fell on the middle of the track and had blood flowing from gashes over her eyes, blinding her. Realizing her danger, she picked herself up and put her body on the side of the tunnel. Afterward, she passed out and lay on the ground for twenty minutes until help arrived.[164]

She was not noticed missing until the train arrived in Rouen. The count contacted the station master, and a search party was sent out. Her injuries were described as "severe…which will necessitate her remaining some considerable time at Roven [sic] before being able to proceed on her journey to Paris."[165]

Not much is known about Marie's life after this accident. Maurice Baring, who was at the British embassy in Paris from 1898 to 1900, recalled seeing Marie on two separate occasions:

> *I got to know a good many French people, and some of those who had been famous in the days of the Second Empire: Madame de Gallifet and Madame de Pourtalès. Madame de Pourtalès had grey hair, but time, which had taken away much from her and stamped her with his pitiless seal, had not taken, and was destined never to take, away the undefinable authority that alone great beauty possesses, and never loses, nor her radiant smile, which would suddenly make her look young.*
>
> *Once at a party at Paris many years after this, at the Jaucourts' house, I again saw Madame de Pourtalès. It was not long before she died. Her hair was, or seemed to be, quite white, and that evening the room was rather dim and lit from the ceiling; her face was powdered and she appeared quite transfigured; the whiteness of her hair and the effect of the light made her face look quite young. You were conscious only of dazzling shoulders, a peerless skin, soft shining eyes, and a magical smile. She put out everyone else in a room. She looked like the photographs of herself taken when she was a young woman. One saw what she must have been, and everybody who was there agreed that here was an instance of the undefinable, undying persistence of great beauty that just when you think it is dead, suddenly blooms afresh and gives you a glimpse of its own past.*
>
> *Reggie Lister told me that he had once asked Madame de Pourtalès what was the greatest compliment that had ever been paid her. She said it was this. Once in summer she had been going out to dinner in Paris. It was rather late in the summer, and a breathless evening, she was sitting in her open carriage, dressed for dinner, waiting for someone in the clear daylight. It was so hot she had only a tulle veil round her shoulders. While she was waiting a workman passed the carriage, and when he saw her he stood and gaped in silence; at last he said: "Christi! que tu es belle!"*[166]

By the turn of the twentieth century, the Pourtalèses had settled in the twenty-five-room Villa Terrarossa near Toscana, Italy, three miles from Florence in what Marie described as "one of the loveliest places in the world."[167]

The one thing Marie was lacking was the sound of little children. She would lament that neither Preston nor Jenny had children, saying, "I seem destined never to be a grandmother."[168]

She was often visited by Preston, who was now a diplomat himself. Her son noticed that Marie was growing "very thin and did not eat much, but still remained a coquette in spite of her wrinkles, and rebelled very hard against growing old." Marie lay on her deathbed for forty-eight hours before dying on January 25, 1908, at Villa Terrarossa, after suffering several years of ill health and depression. On her deathbed, she received the sacraments of the Catholic Church. Interestingly, given how often the false account of her death in Japan was repeated for years around the country, her actual death was not mentioned in her hometown newspaper, the *(Columbia, SC) State*.[169]

Countess Marie de Pourtalès was buried on January 31, 1908, in a cemetery near Florence. The actual location was never made public, probably to keep gawkers away. In a letter to Preston, Count de Pourtalès-Gorgier wrote, "I can say her melancholy and depressed state have contributed much to shorten her days, and she was hurt deeply by the calumnies and criticism of which she was a victim, and for a long time, in spite of my attempts to cheer her morale, she aspired to the rest that death can only procure."[170]

In a letter to Ethland on March 16, 1908, the count told Marie's half sister that he was resting in Tunis to be near his daughter, Jenny, "after the cruel shock and irreparable loss that I have sustained." He also told her, "I am touched by the expression of your sympathy and by the nice things you say about poor Marie, but I am afraid you were still too young when you left her to appreciate all her great qualities."[171]

More sadness would visit the count three years later when his daughter and only child, Marie Pauline Louise de Pourtalès (Jenny), died at the rather young age of forty-one. In Japan in 1898, she had married Antoine von Grubissich de Keresztur, who was first secretary to the Austrian Legion of the Austrian-Hungarian Empire. Later, he became the empire's consul general in Tunis. Given Jenny was a half-American, half-French woman married to a German husband, her death may have been a blessing, as it spared her from what would have been torn loyalties during World War I.[172]

Ethland Feaster spent the rest of her life in Florida. In 1876, she married Dr. Benjamin Rush Wilson of Titusville, Florida, where she remained for the rest of her days. Together they had ten children. She died from a stroke on August 8, 1917, after years of failing health.[173]

Count Arthur Pourtalès-Gorgier outlived his second wife by two decades, dying in 1928. In 1921, Preston Beecher told a cousin, "I frequently see my mother's second husband, the Count de Pourtales, who lives not far from where I do in Paris. He is a charming man, my dearest and most intimate friend…Although about 77 he is a very handsome and distinguished man."[174]

William Preston Beecher enjoyed a successful career in the U.S. and British Diplomatic Corps, serving as U.S. vice and deputy consul in Bordeaux in 1893 and 1894–97 and in Le Havre in 1905–14, U.S. consul in Cognac in 1893–94 and U.S. deputy consul in Le Havre in 1897–99. By the 1920s, he held a position with the Lloyds Agency in Le Havre, France, though he lived in Paris.[175]

In addition to his diplomatic work, Preston Beecher was a journalist-historian of the New York literary scene in 1840s and 1850s. His writings appeared in such prestigious national publications as *Harper's* magazine, the *Nation* and the *Saturday Review*.[176]

Preston married Blanch Louise—an American national born in Argen, France, in 1864—sometime between December 1914 and February 1915. But aside from this, there is no information on Preston's wife or marriage. Preston died in France on September 16, 1939.[177]

Mary's last living half sibling, Julia C. Feaster, married Samuel J. Field, a Confederate veteran, in 1872. They lived in Florida and had six children together. Julia was active in the Daughters of the American Revolution. She died on March 7, 1944.[178]

This 1915 photograph is the only known likeness of Marie's son, Preston Beecher. *Author's collection.*

With the death of Countess Marie de Pourtalès came the end of a life that rivals the life of a heroine in a romance novel, who, not unlike many heroines, was in many ways a victim of her own beauty. How different her life would have been if the Civil War had not come, if she had married Willie Capers or if William Preston had not been killed we can only guess.

Marie may have written her own epitaph fifteen years before her death when she told Ethland:

*God has been very good to me. He has given me a noble, refined, high-souled man to guide and protect me. He has given me a dear sweet loving child [Jenny], and my life is very beautiful and I am very grateful. I never, never think of the past—I live in the present and for the future.*[179]

CHAPTER 5

# Legends and Lies

Usually the death of a person is the end of her story, but not so with Marie or Amelia. Neither leaving South Carolina nor their deaths stopped the stories about them. From the 1870s to the present day, hardly a decade has gone by in which either woman, especially Marie, has not been the subject of or mentioned in passing in a book, pamphlet, newspaper or magazine article.

Most accounts of Marie's life contain gossip, rumors, half-truths and outright lies. Nonetheless, these stories were popular for at least a century and have been taken at face value by "serious" historians. But accuracy of data notwithstanding, it is still remarkable how much was written and said about Marie Boozer Beecher de Pourtalès.

The first author to make note of Marie was none other than General William Tecumseh Sherman himself. In his 1875 *Memoirs*, he mentioned that he "authorized General Howard to send back by this opportunity some of the fugitives who had traveled with his army all the way from Columbia, among whom were Mrs. Feaster and her two beautiful daughters."[180]

"Read This—You'll Like It!" was displayed at the top of the cover of the first "biography" of Marie, 1878's *A Checkered Life: Being a Brief History of the Countess Pourtales, Formerly Miss Marie Boozer of Columbia S.C.* The author, who was listed on the cover as "One Who Knows," was Julian A. Selby (1833–1907), a successful newspaper editor, journalist and historian. Selby would become to Marie what Parson Weems, the man who invented the tale of George Washington and the cherry tree among other tall tales, would be to the first president.[181]

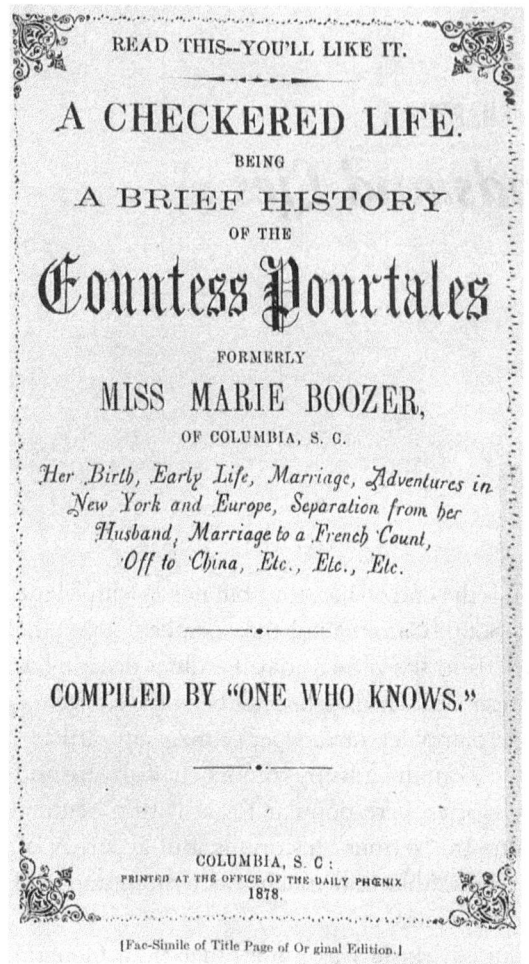

Reproduction of the cover of *A Checkered Life: Being a Brief History of the Countess Pourtales, Formerly Miss Marie Boozer of Columbia S.C.* "Read this—you'll like it," promised the caption at the top of the 1878 pamphlet written by "One Who Knows." *Image courtesy of the Walker Local and Family History Center, Richland Library, Columbia, South Carolina.*

The book is the only known detailed account of Amelia's early life, though Selby incorrectly refers to David Boozer as a doctor, a mistake that would be passed on by other scholars. Selby, the editor of the *Columbia Phoenix* (publishers and printers of the text), was a former neighbor of the Feasters and certainly knew the two women. The parts of the twenty-five-page booklet detailing Amelia's and Marie's lives before the Civil War and during their stay in Columbia are believed to be mostly accurate.[182]

But calling Boozer a doctor is in no way the biggest factual error in the book. Once Selby starts writing about what happened to the ladies after they left Columbia, the book completely sinks into the realm of fiction. There are fabricated tales, such as Marie going to California and while en route being courted by both Brigham Young and his son, Brigham Young Jr. According to this story, the son of the Mormon leader kidnapped her, but she was recused by the U.S. Cavalry. After this misadventure, Marie continued to California and then on to New York. Selby also includes a letter reportedly written by Marie from China, though in reality Marie was in Japan at the time. (Theoretically,

Julian Selby, Columbia, South Carolina publisher/newspaperman, aka "One Who Knows," was the first to besmirch Marie's name, allegedly in a failed attempt to wreck her second marriage. *Image courtesy of the Walker Local and Family History Center, Richland Library, Columbia, South Carolina.*

Marie could have visited China while in Japan, but there is no known record of her doing so.)

Selby also includes tales of Marie in the Russian court creating all kinds of scandal. He also links Marie with Cora Pearl (1835?–1886), a notorious English-born Parisian courtesan. Though she is now all but forgotten, Pearl in her prime was the Madonna or Lady Gaga of her day, and the subject of many articles and books. Pearl once went to a gala with her hair dyed to match her carriage. On another occasion, she dyed her dog's fur to match her dress. Pearl was also known to arrive at parties attended by Europe's elite scantily clad or naked.[183]

It is very possible that Pearl did enjoy the company of a Countess de Pourtalès. If so, it was not Marie, but one of the previously mentioned women who shared the title. Furthermore, at the time that Marie arrived in Paris, Pearl's life as a courtesan was all but over due to too many scandals and financial problems. Thus, while they could have met, it seems unlikely that they did.

Undoubtedly, Selby, being a newspaper publisher, would have known about Pearl and might have assumed that a story involving the courtesan and

Though all but forgotten today, Miss Cora Pearl was one of the most famous and scandalous women in all of late-nineteenth-century Europe. Marie was often falsely linked with her. *Author's collection.*

a Countess de Pourtalès would be about Marie Boozer. However, Selby's intentions may not have been sincere.

Elizabeth Boatwright Coker speculated that *A Checkered Life* may have been a deliberate attempt by Selby to sabotage Marie's second marriage. The motivation, according to Mrs. Coker, is that Selby and Amelia were in an affair that was discovered by a disapproving Marie, causing the two lovers to break it off. Exactly how or where Mrs. Coker reached this conclusion is unclear, but reading between the lines in the way Selby talks glowingly about Amelia and harshly about Marie, this theory is plausible.[184]

As it will be seen, Selby's account was taken at face value for over a century by serious scholars, though his identity as "One Who Knows" was not publicly confirmed until the late 1950s. The two women who chose to use Marie's life as the basis of their historical novels, Mrs. Coker and Mrs. Nell Graydon, all but discredit Selby's booklet, though it obviously influenced their works. Mrs. Graydon, the author of the 1958 novel *Another Jezebel*, reprinted several of Selby's claims but added, "This writer is convinced there is little truth in them."[185]

Mrs. Coker included Selby's "China letter" in *La Belle* and presented it as fact. But in an unpublished 1974 fact-based biography of Marie's life, Mrs. Coker dismissed it. "None of *Checkered Life* washes," she wrote. "The whole book is obvious with errors from start to finish should anybody bother to check out." She also came to the conclusion that the China letter was a "phony."[186]

Writing under the alias "Felix Old Boy," the highly respected University of South Carolina professor Yates Snowden expanded Selby's work and reproduced it in 1915. *Author's collection.*

Strangely enough, in 1905, when Selby published his book *Memorabilia and Anecdotal Reminiscences of Columbia S.C. and Incidents Connected Therewith*, an excellent serious look at Columbia's history, published under his own name, he made no mention of Amelia or Marie. While it is possible that this omission was the result of Selby's feeling guilty for what he had previously done, it is more likely that he may have been worried that mentioning Amelia and Marie in this work might cause someone to identify him as "One Who Knows."[187]

*A Checkered Life* was republished in 1915 with additional material as *The Countess Pourtales*. The author of the new material, credited as "Felix Old Boy" was Yates Snowden (1858–1933), the distinguished chairman of the University of South Carolina's Department of History. Noted for his introduction of advanced classes of the French Revolution and the Reconstruction era, he was affectionately called "the Incarnation of the Old South" because he wore a black cape and was considered handsome, witty and charming.[188]

The additions included a new introduction and a supposed account from a San Francisco newspaper. It also linked Marie with Kilpatrick, citing E.L. Wells's *A Morning Call on General Kilpatrick*, which originally appeared in the *Southern Historical Society Papers* in March 1884.[189]

Snowden obviously knew what he was getting into, as he offered a caveat in his introduction: "The main facts set forth in this pamphlet as to Marie's birth and early life in Columbia are correct." He further stated, "But the narrative by "One Who Knows" incorrect though it be in occasional details is of absorbing interest; pity that the whole life story could not be procured and published."[190]

Of course, the question one has to ask is why would a highly respected and distinguished history professor lower himself to republish such a tawdry bit of gossip? In a January 2, 1916 letter to his close friend and correspondent John Bennett of Charleston, Snowden claimed:

> *I had nothing to do with the republication of old Julian Selby's "grind," though I had a copy of the original pamphlet in my collection. James Holmes, a fine fellow, who has had unmerciful disaster follow fast, &c., and young Selby thought they could make some Xmas money by republishing the stuff. Jim complained that it would not make a big enough pamphlet for their price,* one dollar; *& I said I would write an introduction: hence the more or less damphool "Study in Scarlet" & the "foreword" from Dr. Warren, to give it an ethical, highly moral touch! As a matter of fact I have* bought *two copies, and stranger still,* paid *for them.*[191]

Snowden closed his letter by stating, "I too have heard that Marie Boozer (Pourtales) was 'beheaded, by order of the Mikado'! But; who knows?"[192]

Still, Snowden himself realized the consequences of being attached to the booklet. In December 1915, when he sent a copy of the booklet to a friend, Snowden included a note saying, "I am sending you, under other cover, a pamphlet entitled *The Countess Pourtales*; pray God, Mrs. Bennett does not look at it." He added, "Keep your mouth shut."[193]

Snowden had reason to be concerned. When Bennett showed the pamphlet to a mutual female friend, Snowden responded, "That dear lady, I fear, thinks *my mind runs* on that kind of 'literature.' It doesn't; you know *it doesn't!*"[194]

While the exact sales figures are unknown, it appears that Snowden's reprint sold well, perhaps better than Selby's original. Snowden's work can be readily found in many South Carolina libraries, while the 1878 version is very rare. This also suggests that Selby's slanders had started to be forgotten until Snowden brought them back into the public eye. Consider that Edwin J. Scott's *Random Recollections of a Long Life: 1806–1876*, published just six years after Selby's booklet, makes no mentions of the Feaster store or residence in this otherwise detailed description of what downtown Columbia was like in the nineteenth century. Consequently, Snowden may be as guilty as Selby for propagating falsehoods about Marie.[195]

Edward Wells, a South Carolina Confederate cavalry man whose two firsthand accounts of South Carolinians in the Civil War are considered among the best, referred to Marie in 1888's *A Sketch of the Charleston Light Dragoons*. He does not refer to Marie by name but gave a very interesting account of her and an alleged misadventure:[196]

> *A Confederate detachment noticed the track of wheels looking very unlike the broad ruts left by artillery, or wagon-trains. These impressions were evidently those made by a light carriage, and not by some coarse "buggy" stolen from the country people. Then there arose much excitement among certain of the "Dragoons"; they opened in full cry on the trail in fact. Indeed there were not wanting some older fellows, who smiled and looked interested.*
>
> *To make clear the cause of all this it will only be necessary to give this explanation. At Columbia, prior to February 17th, might have been seen, any day and many times a day, a certain very pretty woman, "dressed to kill," driving in her carriage, her dainty little feet rarely touching the pavement except when she was entering a shop. She did not belong to the* derni monde, *or the "Dragoons," being properly behaved young men, of course would not have been acquainted with her; yet it must be confessed her paternity, like that of some of the most famous Goddesses of Mythology, was involved in much obscurity. This damsel, under her mother's wing, left Columbia with Sherman's army, and afterwards made an advantageous marriage at* [sic] *the North with a relative of a noted Brooklyn preacher, who was by profession a philanthropist, in practice a philogynist.*
>
> *After skirmishing a little while in the borderland of Gotham's society, she figured as defendant in a law suit; then indulged in pistol-practice in the streets, lodging a derringer-bullet among the back teeth of one of the* jeunesse doree, *and finished up by marrying a second time a titled foreigner of Latin extraction. Now these wheel-tracks were supposed to have been made by the carriage of this beautiful Helen of Troy, and she herself was believed to be in Kilpatrick's camp, where unprotected females were wont to find a haven. The cause of the excitement among the boys, and their elders, too, probably needs no further explanation.*[197]

The *Anderson (SC) Intelligence* published on November 6, 1884, "A Columbia Woman's Romance," which was reprinted from an unnamed New York newspaper. A similar tale was published in the *Daily Morning Astorian (OR)* on July 19, 1885. The latter is interesting because the unnamed author claims to be someone who knew Marie yet misspells her married name as "Portallis." Given that much of the piece reads like Selby's account, including the Brigham Young connection, it may have been the work of the Columbia author.[198]

It ended with this fanciful tale regarding Marie's alleged misadventures in Japan:

> [A jilted Japanese lover] *reported her to the Mikado of the empire and asked for her arrest, then he hired assassins to behead her, and throw her body into a ditch. Such barbarity seems hardly credible in this enlightened age, and we hope the story may be incorrect. Of her death we are assured by persons from Japan, and if all the horrors attributed to the manner of her death prove true, it certainly is the most tragic ending to one of the most eventful lives ever published.*

Of course, Marie was still very much alive and well.[199]

On February 25, 1894, the *(Atlanta, GA) Constitution* published "The Countess Percele [*sic*]—The Famous and Notorious Adventures of a South Carolina Beauty" by David Augustus Dickert. Dickert (1844–1917) was a former Confederate officer best remembered for his often-cited history of Kershaw's Brigade. Though he was commonly called "colonel," it was only a term of affection, as he ended the war with the rank of captain. Despite having very little formal education, he spent his postwar years writing a number of articles for his local newspaper in addition to his book.[200]

Dickert began his piece by writing, "'The Countess Perceles has lost her head.' Such is the news that comes from far-off Japan." He then asks, "And who was the Countess Perceles? Who this distant princess that we in the south should be interested in her sad ending? At one time the whole state of South Carolina would have listened with bated breath to catch one word of this famous beauty."

He then goes into Marie's early life (calling her "Mary"), in the process incorrectly stating that Jacob Feaster had no children of his own. He further shows his ignorance of facts by stating that the IX[th] U.S. Army Corps led by Major General Edward Ord occupied Columbia and that the general personally befriended Marie and Amelia. In reality, the IX[th] Corps was not a part of Sherman's army during its march through South Carolina; it was in Virginia during the march. Nor was General Ord ever the IX[th] Corps commander or in Columbia; he commanded the Department of North Carolina.[201]

The article recounts the tales of Marie in Russia and Japan. Dickert concluded his piece with "away in foreign lands, friendless and alone, Mary [sic] Boozer, Countess Percele [sic], paid the penalty of a wayward and wicked life by being brought to the block."[202]

Mrs. Coker believed that Dickert's motivation for this slanderous piece of writing was that he was a would-be suitor of Marie, whose affections were rebuffed. As it shall be seen, this would not be his last attack on Marie.[203]

Dickert's article gained a response from a writer identified only as "C.D.M." whose article "A Fair Adventuress" was published in the *(Atlanta, GA) Constitution* on March 16, 1894. C.D.M. starts out by saying that there are so many discrepancies in Dickert's piece that "as a native South Carolinian and a citizen of Columbia I feel called upon to give a true version."[204]

Despite having little formal education, D.A. Dickert became one of South Carolina's most prolific writers after the Civil War. Marie's supposed rejection of his affections led him to write at least three slanderously false accounts of her life and death. *Image courtesy of the Walker Local and Family History Center, Richland Library, Columbia, South Carolina.*

The author claimed to have known Amelia and Marie, and he provides some information on them that does not appear anywhere else. C.D.M. rebuffed the claims that Marie was beheaded and involved in the Russian jewel scandal, though he cites Selby's "letter from Marie" as proof that she was still alive. He ended his piece by asking, "Who can say in the most sin-seared heart some longing for better things do not lie, and that Marie Boozer, Countess de Pourtales, may not yet become a respectable woman."[205]

On September 9, 1894, readers of the *St. Paul (MN) Daily Globe* were treated to a front-page story entitled "Six Adventuresses, Women Who by Beauty or Wit Ensnared and Fleeced Notable Men." One of those six was Marie, who was depicted in a surprisingly accurate illustration. However, that would prove to be about the only accurate thing in this slanderous account of Marie's life.[206]

The uncredited author wrote:

> *The Countess Pourtales, an American beheaded by the order of the Mikado of Japan without the affair creating any international sensation, was the most sensationalist adventuress of her day; and although she flourished along with several others, her career was much swifter—like her death. The lovely countess began life as Marie Boozer, of South Carolina. She married several times, shot at her husbands, either killing them or making them sue for divorce papers, and then she went to Paris…*[There] *Mary Boozer met the young Count Pourtales and married him. They were sent to Japan on a diplomatic mission, and very soon the count got into a duel about his wife's behavior and was killed.*[207]

The rather fantastical account goes on to say that Marie returned to Paris and married another French officer and the two were returned to Japan, where "in a month the ex-countess had created so many difficulties, caused so many fatal duels and captured the hearts of so many married men, that the Mikado 'got mad' as we say here, and ordered her head be cut off. The order was promptly executed, and there was rejoicing in the royal palace."[208]

As previously mentioned, the *Chicago Tribune* of August 27, 1898, actually published a tale that defended Marie, calling the tales about Marie in Japan "Fairy tales for they are nothing else" and noting that they disgusted and annoyed the count.[209]

Colonel James Gibbes mentioned Amelia and Marie in his 1902 pamphlet *Who Burnt Columbia?* Gibbes, who was mayor of Columbia right after Sherman left the city, repeated Selby's false claim that Marie was one of "the parties that were mixed up with the Crown Prince of Russia, a few years ago, and the loss of his mother's diamonds." This apparently led to Marie being expelled from Russia.[210]

Marie and Amelia were also gossiped about in *South Carolina Women in the Confederacy*, published by the South Carolina Division of the United Daughters of the Confederacy the following year.[211]

In 1905, Mary Chesnut's firsthand account of the Civil War, *A Diary from Dixie*, was published. Though Mrs. Chesnut made several references to Marie and Amelia in her original diary, they were excised from the first edition.[212]

In 1949, a new expanded and annotated edition of *A Diary* was published. Novelist Ben Ames Williams reedited the book to improve its narrative flow. This edition included Mrs. Chesnut's comments about Marie, though she was only mentioned as "Boozer" while Amelia was referred to as "Mrs. F."[213]

## Legends and Lies

It was not until 1981 with *Mary Chesnut's Civil War*, edited by C. Vann Woodward, that Mrs. Chesnut's thoughts on Marie and Amelia were presented in their full, uncensored form. Woodward, who won the 1982 Pulitzer Prize for History for this work, produced a companion piece in 1984, *The Private Mary Chesnut*, containing more previously unpublished materials, though this book contained nothing about Marie or Amelia.[214]

On June 6, 1905, the *Washington Post* published an article about Marie and her husband. In the article, the paper recapped the death of the count's first wife and the train accident that almost killed Marie. It also recounted the gossip about Marie's flirtations with Lloyd Phoenix while she was married to Beecher and the tales about Japan.[215]

In 1906, several newspapers carried an illustrated article entitled "Women as Soldiers of Fortune," written and illustrated by a person identified only as Terison.[216]

"Soldiers of fortune among men is not uncommon," the piece stated, "But when a woman is cursed with the same spirit she leaves a wake of trouble that involves many other men and women. She must use men to secure those things for her which she herself is unable to secure. Men must be her tools, made to do her bidding under the influence of her fascination."[217]

Marie is the first person discussed in this article and the "biography" of her is basically a rehash of the 1884 account of her life. The piece also includes a drawing of Marie shooting a man and ends with her execution in Japan. "The inside story has never been told," wrote Terison, "but that there must be one is proven by the fact that the whole matter was hushed up and forgotten. Three nations might have been involved in so rash an order but were not."[218]

Given the date of this article, just two years before Marie's actual death, and the national exposure it had, combined with Count de Pourtalès's comment that depression over the critical things that were written about her, one cannot help but wonder if this article were the thing that pushed Marie over the edge and contributed to her death?

A year and a half after Marie's death, Dickert wrote about his would-be love interest in "The Sorceress of the Congaree" for the *Newberry (SC) Herald & News*. "The Sorceress" is full of factual errors. Dickert claimed that Amelia was widowed and that she and Marie had two troops of cavalry for escorts through the Carolinas. He also claimed that Amelia tried to get Washington to give her $30,000. Dickert spared no venom toward Marie. He again told the tales of scandals in Russia and Japan.[219]

As previously mentioned, Dickert also wrote an obituary for Marie that was reprinted in the September 18, 1927 issue of the *Augusta (GA) Chronicle*. In this wildly imaginative piece, Dickert claimed that Congress rushed through a bill to give Marie $10 million for aiding POWs to escape and her personal losses when Columbia burned. (Ironically, in his 1894 account Dickert had the correct amount of $10,000.) He further claimed that after her divorce, Marie went to Europe with Cora Pearl with letters of introduction from U.S. government officials.[220]

The next writer to discuss Marie was Robert de Treville Lawrence, a former Confederate soldier, who penned "The Much Married Miss Mary Boozer," which appeared in the January 1921 issue of *Confederate Veteran*, the official publication of the United Confederate Veterans.[221]

Lawrence admitted that he did not know Marie personally but "saw her frequently while a student at the South Carolina College." He further added, "I cannot vouch for all of the statements in the following short narrative of her career, yet, though they appear more like fiction than facts, they were currently reported and accepted as true by all who were interested in the history of Miss Boozer from their knowledge of her early life."[222]

Compared to most early accounts of Marie's life, Lawrence's version is more accurate than most, though he seems to have borrowed from Wells's account. Unlike Selby and Dickert, Lawrence seems to have had no personal vendetta against Marie and freely admits that there are parts of the story he cannot vouch for. However, he misidentifies David Boozer as an "uncle" and cites Shelby's account of Marie in Japan.[223]

Lawrence ends his article on a wistful note:

> *Thus ended the romantic career of Mary Boozer, a woman from whose intrigues no one could escape if she esteemed him of sufficient importance to warrant her attack. What became of her stepfather after she left Columbia or of her mother after she left Philadelphia no one seemed to have thought of sufficient interest to report, so wonderful was the short life and tragic end of their daughter.*[224]

In 1929, James Franklin Williams published the pamphlet *Old and New Columbia*, still regarded as one of the best firsthand reminisces of the city. Williams, who may have known Marie and Amelia personally, wrote that Marie "was a notorious character, and her mother was equally as bad. They were both beautiful women, but that does not go far if it has not the character to back it up."[225]

In 1936, Francis Butler Simkins and James Welch Patton wrote *The Women of the Confederacy*, an overview of Southern women during the war. Their study cited Gibbes's *Who Burned Columbia?* account of Marie, called "Mary" by the authors, who described her as a "golden hair[ed]…young woman of marvelous beauty, wit, and charms who had espoused the Union cause early in the war." It also included the before mentioned fake obituary written by D.A. Dickert.[226]

The Federally funded Works Projects Administration's *The WPA Guide to the Palmetto State*, published in 1941, called Marie "a dubious symbol of Yankee victory" who "drew down upon herself the wrath of the citizens."[227]

The guidebook, apparently drawing heavily from Selby's work, went on to state:

> Marie and her mother lived in Columbia, where they entertained lavishly in an attempt to get into "society." Popular with Union officers, she married one of them in North Carolina. In her travels she associated with Cora Pearl, Louis Napoleon's friend, and later her name was linked with a scandal concerning Russian jewels. Later she became the wife of Count Pourtales, a member of the French Embassy in Washington, whose relatives thereupon had him sent to the legation in China. There Marie married a Japanese nobleman, who, because [of] other infidelities, it is asserted, had her beheaded.[228]

In 1956 Dr. John G. Barrett's *Sherman's March Through the Carolinas* was published. The first scholarly and in-depth look at this historic event included several references to Marie and Amelia, linking Marie with Kilpatrick. Unfortunately, he used Selby's work as his reference.[229]

In the late 1950s, Marie's life became the subject of two historical romance novels. The first one, *Another Jezebel: A Yankee Spy in South Carolina* by Nell S. Graydon (1893–1986), was published in 1958. The title was inspired by the Bette Davis film *Jezebel*, which was based on a play of the same name by Owen Davis Sr. The name "Jezebel" is taken from the Old Testament account found in the two Books of Kings about an unscrupulous, manipulative, pagan-worshipping queen who was the power behind the throne. By the nineteenth century, the term had come to refer to "an impudent, daring, vicious woman"—certainly an apt description of Amelia.[230]

Mrs. Graydon was a native of North Carolina who became interested in South Carolina's history during her vacations at her Edisto Island summer home. After writing a series of newspaper articles, she published her first book, *Tales of Edisto*, in 1955. The popular success of this tome led her to a writing career. *Another Jezebel* was her second work. She returned to nonfiction

THE SCANDALOUS LIVES OF CAROLINA BELLES MARIE BOOZER AND AMELIA FEASTER

Though the book is mostly a work of fiction, author/historian Nell S. Graydon included several actual events in her 1958 novel. Mrs. Graydon later came to regret ever writing it. *Author's collection.*

with *Tales of Beaufort* (1963), *Tales of Columbia* (1964) and *South Carolina Ghost Tales* (1969). In 1967, she wrote her second and last historical novel, *Elizabeth of Wapoo: A Tale of Indigo*, based on the life of Elizabeth Lucas Pinckney. In later years, she wrote books about gardening and cooking.[231]

Mrs. Graydon researched Amelia's and Marie's lives, creating a work of fiction that was based on fact from Amelia's marriage to Burton to her leaving Columbia. She also included a fact-based postscript dealing with Marie's life as a countess. She would later write, "Why I even wrote [the book] I do not know—but the story did intrigue me."[232]

The book was published regionally by the R.L. Bryan Company of Columbia, South Carolina, in both hardback and paperback editions. Eugene Sloan, a critic for the *State* newspaper in Columbia called the book "delightful." However, Mrs. Graydon took a different view of her work. The year after it was published, she wrote, "I do not want that book republished. Fiction to live must be great—and no one knows better than I know *Another Jezebel* is not great." Mrs. Graydon got her wish, as no other editions were published.[233]

The next year, 1959, the second and arguably most famous fictionalized account of Marie's life was published: Elizabeth Boatwright Coker's *La Belle: A Novel Based on the Life of the Notorious Southern Belle, Marie Boozer, Who Rode Away With Sherman's Army After the Burning of Columbia*, published nationally by E.P. Dutton & Co., Inc., of New York.

Mrs. Coker (1909–1993) was the granddaughter of James Lide Coker, founder of Coker College in Hartsville, South Carolina. The Darlington, South Carolina native graduated from Converse College in Spartanburg, where she served as the editor of the school's literary paper and won prizes for her poetry. After college, she struck out for the Big Apple and was on the verge of starting a career with the *New York Times* when the Great Depression struck, forcing her to return to the Palmetto State. Despite the setback, she continued to write, receiving praise from Robert Frost for one of her stories.[234]

Mrs. Coker published her first book *Daughters of Strangers* in 1950; it made the *New York Times* bestsellers list and stayed there for six months. She would go on to write the historical novels *The Day of the Peacock* (1952), *India Allan* (1953), *The Big Drum* (1957), *Lady Rich* (1963), *The Bees* (1968), *Blood Red Roses* (1977) and *The Grasshopper King* (1981). She was the recipient of numerous literary awards.[235]

At the beginning of *La Belle*, Mrs. Coker waxes poetical:

> *Like all great beauties Marie Boozer was a combination of classic features, exquisite flesh, and that ineffable essence, or natural perfume, without*

Elizabeth Boatwright Coker, one of South Carolina's most successful and prolific authors of the late twentieth century, tried and failed twice to produce a nonfiction book about Marie's life. *Author's collection.*

*which no woman, whatever her physical perfection, can take her place in beauty ranks.*

*The truth about Marie, as always with the lovely and the lost, has been so lacquered by gossip, legend and anecdote that it has been difficult to separate the real woman from the mythological one. Thus while seeking out the mirror view of her I could never fail to be influenced by the spell she cast. To this day people in Columbia still speak of Marie and her mother with as much current curiosity, envy, admiration and opprobrium as they do of the fiery General Sherman who once visited their City. It is almost as if these handsome ladies had just passed by in their crystal coach.*[236]

Like Mrs. Graydon, Mrs. Coker did as much research into Marie's life as possible. She would later admit to spending two years looking for information on Amelia without too much success. Eventually, she "realized I had far too few facts and too many conclusions." Thus, she turned it into a novel, though she included a bibliography with the caveat: "My 'real life' information about Marie has come from many and varied sources, not all of them reliable." She also cited verbatim Marie's adoption papers and David Boozer's will.[237]

To try to fill in the gaps, she approached Mrs. Graydon in 1957 (both women were aware of the other's project), suggesting that they might want to share each other's research. However, both women were in a race to get their book out first and were very competitive on their research, thus Mrs. Graydon rejected the idea. She later told Mrs. Coker, "When I received your letter in 1957 I had nearly finished my manuscript and assumed obligations to another or I would have left the story to you."[238]

Of the two novels, *La Belle* is clearly the better written one, though like *Another Jezebel*, *La Belle* is guilty of serious historical errors, most of which are due to Coker's taking Selby's account at face value. In a letter to Marie's niece, Mrs. Coker stated that she interviewed John Selby, the ninety-year-old son of Julian Selby, who insisted "that his father's book was absolutely true."[239]

Mrs. Coker concluded her book with a section entitled "What Happened After." In it, she reprinted the "China letter," a tale that Mary divorced the count and married the caliph of Baghdad, who was so afraid that she would grow weary of him and leave that he had the tendons in her heels cut and she was carried on a gold velvet cushion by two "Nubian eunuchs." Eventually, she grew so fat that it took four eunuchs to carry her.[240]

Mrs. Coker then reprinted the Dickert "obituary" and concluded by saying that all such tales are rubbish, pointing out that several European sources listed Marie as a countess and gave the true date and place of her death.[241]

The novel received good reviews both nationally and in England. The *New York Herald-Tribune* called *La Belle* an "engrossing sidelight at history," while Chapman J. Milling in the *State* wrote, "It has a fascination which will not let one put it down."[242]

*La Belle* would go through four printings: the original 1959 hardcover version, a 1960 Dell paperback edition, a 1976 paperback edition from Mocking Bird Books of Atlanta and a 1978 paperback edition by Bantam Books.

It is interesting to note the different covers that the four editions had. The 1959 one features an alluring blonde woman in an oval picture frame. The 1960 paperback edition shows a blonde woman in a seductive embrace with a Confederate officer. The 1976 edition features a disheveled blonde woman with a 1970s hairstyle holding a Confederate flag with the famed *Harper's Weekly* illustration on the burning of Columbia as a back drop, done in a stylistic manner. For the 1978 edition, a young, sweet and innocent smiling

Marie comes across as a femme fatal on the 1958 cover of the first edition of the novel *La Belle*, published by E.P. Dutton & Co., Inc., of New York. *Author's collection.*

The 1978 Bantam Books edition of *La Belle* has Amelia as a conniving woman and Marie as an innocent young girl on its cover. This cover does the most accurate job of capturing the spirit of the novel of all the editions of *La Belle* published to date. *Author's collection.*

blonde girl is shown with a devious looking brunette woman, smoking a cigar behind her. The cover also features two older men and a Confederate flag in the bottom left corner.

On the other hand, the covers for *Another Jezebel* just show a woman and a plantation house drawn in a simple, minimalist modern style.

Mrs. Elizabeth Battle of Florida, the then sixty-nine-year-old daughter of Ethland, wrote to both Mrs. Graydon and Mrs. Coker. Her letters caught both authors off guard, as neither one had any idea that there were any living relatives of Marie or Amelia. In her letter to Mrs. Graydon, Mrs. Battle wrote, "Believe me Mrs. Graydon we are not offended by your portrayal of [Amelia] in your book. After reading your book I told my sister immediately that it was without an obsession against anyone, and you had a gentle touch." Though she felt, "knowing what a wonderful, intelligent person my mother was, I feel that her own mother could never have been the type of person some writers have tried to make her."[243]

Still Mrs. Graydon felt bad about what she had done. "I have tried in my writing 'never' by word or insinuation to publish anything that would bring unhappiness. It is with deep regret I learned too late, that the book *Another Jezebel* brought sorrow to a group of fine people. I think it has upset me now more than anything that has ever happened to me."[244]

However, in letters to Mrs. Coker, Mrs. Battle admitted that she did not like either book and especially hated *La Belle*, calling it "vulgar" and stating that it "has left some scars." In one vicious letter, Mrs. Battle called the novel "full of untruths" and suggested, "Won't you in the future try to write more kindly if your characters are from real life and save others that 'mental anguish!'"[245]

She added, "Mrs. Graydon surely feels badly about writing *Another Jezebel* and is anxious to do all she can [to set the record straight] and as a member of the [South] Carolina Historical Society [she] is writing a piece to be put on record so others will not be mistaken."[246]

Mrs. Battle had shared with both Mrs. Graydon and Mrs. Coker copies of letters from and about Marie. Mrs. Graydon made them available to the *State* newspaper in Columbia, which published them as "Living Descendant's Letter Sheds Light" on November 1, 1959, and "Heroine of Mrs. Graydon's Book Writes of Her Travels Abroad During the 1800's [sic]" on February 23, 1960.[247]

There is no record of Mrs. Battle being upset with Mrs. Graydon's publishing the letters in the newspaper. However, her relationship with Mrs. Coker had deteriorated so badly that she started sending letters to

Mrs. Coker and her publisher, Scott Bartlett, editor in chief of E.P. Dutton, refusing permission to publish the letters in future editions of *La Belle*. This led Bartlett to call Mrs. Battle "an irritated and irritating person." During their heated exchange of letters, Mrs. Coker informed Mrs. Battle that since the letters in question had been published in the *State* newspaper, they were now in the public domain and could be cited without her permission. To her credit, Mrs. Battle eventually apologized to Mrs. Coker.[248]

Despite the criticisms and misgivings, neither author could turn her back on Marie. Mrs. Graydon in her 1964 book *Tales of Columbia* devoted a section to Marie's life. In it she refers to Marie as "Mary," calling her "one of the most beautiful girls in the state." Mrs. Graydon's account takes up about two and a half pages and is pretty accurate. She does not go into a great deal about Amelia's or Marie's postwar life, other than to say, "Many lurid stories were told in Columbia of the mother and daughter. Resentment of the mother's Northern sympathies was undoubtedly responsible for some of them."[249]

Meanwhile, Mrs. Coker decided to put the lies and legends about Marie to rest once and for all. In 1974, she prepared a serious, fact-based biography of Marie entitled *Sandal or Scandal: Being the True Story of the Countess Pourtales, Formerly Miss Marie Boozer of Columbia S.C.* with Mrs. Coker going by the nom de plume of "Elizabeth Old Girl," an obvious nod to Dr. Snowden.[250]

Mrs. Coker's text blasts previously published negative accounts of Marie's life and offers some very interesting insights into her real story. Unfortunately, Mrs. Coker's manuscript is not annotated, so some of her sources are unknown.[251]

*Sandal or Scandal* was never published. Instead, Mrs. Coker wrote "La Belle Marie: The Final Chapter," which appeared in the November 1976 issue of *Sandlapper: The Magazine of South Carolina*.[252]

In the article, which may or may not have been timed to coincide with the republication of the *La Belle*, Mrs. Coker confessed to being unable to find out anything more about Marie's life until the novel was in the galley proof stage. It was only after the book was published that information started falling into Mrs. Coker's hands.[253]

Some of it was obviously false. One woman, whose mother had gone to school with Marie, told Mrs. Coker that "Marie eventually married the sultan of Turkey. Jealous of Marie, the sultan cut her heel strings so she could never run away from him. She grew enormously fat and was carried about on a golden cushion by four handsome Greek eunuchs."[254]

Another told her, "Marie went off to Africa and became a Zulu. The Zulus who treasured her, reluctantly did what was necessary to keep her forever. The 'somebody' swore he'd personally seen Marie's shrunken head with all its glory of golden hair on a tribal altar."[255]

Mrs. Coker dismissed these tales and included some family letters regarding Marie's true fate and the eyewitness account from Maurice Baring. "So *actually* Marie died surrounded by pomp and circumstance and love in a swansdown bed in a bona fide castle," wrote Mrs. Coker.[256]

She concluded her piece by saying:

> *I'm not sure I would have dared become so familiar with Marie as I did had I been aware of her grand finale. Not knowing whether it was the golden cushion or the shrunken head or the Mikado's axe-man kept me racing on with breathless anticipation. But what a joyous triumph to have my hunch all long vindicated: Marie Boozer of Columbia, South Carolina, was La Belle and hardly a hussy at all!*[257]

Another narrative of Marie's life was told in James Dunwoody Jones's firsthand narrative published as "A Guard at Andersonville" in the February 1964 issue of *Civil War Times Illustrated*.[258]

Jones claimed that between her marriages to Beecher and de Pourtalès, Marie was involved with a rich Brazilian living in Paris. Marie allegedly spent all of the man's money, forcing him to beg for a living until he shot himself in the head. Jones also insisted that de Pourtalès kicked out Marie after she "squandered his fortune" and that she wound up in Siam (present-day Thailand), where she was put in the harem of the viceroy. Despite the designation of "favorite" of the harem, she eventually had an affair with a French sailor. When the viceroy discovered this, he had her beheaded. Jones quipped, "Mary Boozer was not the first girl to lose her head over a sailor. Nor the last."[259]

Another serious attempt at exposing the truth about Marie's and Amelia's lives was made by Mary Elizabeth Boozer, a distant relative of "Big Dave," in 1970, when her *Boozer Family of South Carolina* was published. The well-researched book made it very clear that contrary to the two novels, Marie's stepfather was not a doctor.[260]

In 1980, Marie's legend was treated as a serious matter in Burke Davis's *Sherman's March*, published nationally by Random House. Davis, who did not use footnotes, took the Selby account at its word and also included accounts from *South Carolina Women in the Confederacy*. He also repeated that Marie and Kilpatrick were lovers and that she was with him at the Battle of Monroe's Crossroads in North Carolina. In addition, Davis claimed that Marie became an Asian concubine.[261]

Charles Royster, in his critically acclaimed 1991 book, *The Destructive War*, mentioned Marie in passing when discussing Sherman's departure from Columbia: "Elegantly displaying herself in a huge landau, the most beautiful white woman in Columbia, Marie Boozer—one of those a black man described as 'not real ladies, but second-hand ladies'—...found for herself among Sherman's young officers a husband who would do until she met a wealthy New York businessman."[262]

While it is clear that Royster cites Colonel Gibbes's pamphlet, Royster's way of doing footnotes and the lack of a proper bibliography makes it difficult to tell whom, if anyone else, he used for this passage in *The Destructive War*.

John Hammond Moore mentioned Marie and Amelia in passing in what is the definitive history of the Greater Columbia area to date, 1993's *Columbia & Richland County: A South Carolina Community, 1740–1990*, citing Williams's work in the footnotes.[263]

In 1996, Samuel J. Martin, a resident of Hilton Head, South Carolina, wrote *Kill-Cavalry: The Life of Union General Hugh Judson Kilpatrick*, a very interesting book about Sherman's colorful and controversial cavalry chief. Unfortunately, he took Selby's booklet at face value and linked Marie and Kilpatrick. He also took Burke Davis's account as completely accurate.[264]

I added to the legend of Marie Boozer with the before mentioned "Lurid Legends of a Wayward Woman," published in *Civil War Magazine* in August 1997. It was intended to be as factually based as possible, emphasizing the use of Mrs. Graydon's and Mrs. Coker's later writings, and the myths and legends were acknowledged only as such. Unfortunately, I fell for the trap of linking Marie with Kilpatrick, but aside from that major faux pas, the article remained the most complete and honest biography of Marie to that date.[265]

That same year, Kenneth Belew prepared for the U.S. Army Eighteenth Air Borne Corps and North Carolina's Fort Bragg *Cavalry Clash in the Sandhills: The Battle of Monroe's Crossroads, North Carolina, 10 March, 1865*. This book was written under the auspices of the U.S. Department of the Interior, the National Park Service, the Midwest Archeological Center and the Southeast Archeological Center. It, too, lists Marie as being with Kilpatrick, and as of 2014, the online version of this tale on the National Parks Service website still contains this incorrect information.[266]

Marie entered the twenty-first century in Eric J. Wittenberg's *The Battle of Monroe's Crossroads and the Civil War's Final Campaign*. In it he included an appendix of who was with Kilpatrick at the North Carolina battle, which puts to rest once and for all the story that Marie and Kilpatrick had an affair, pointing out that the two were nowhere near each other from Columbia to Fayetteville.[267]

I have kept Amelia's and Marie's memories alive in the second decade of the twenty-first century by mentioning them, factually, in 2011's *Columbia Civil War Landmarks* and 2012's *A Carnival of Destruction: Sherman's Invasion of South Carolina*. With this book, I intend to say a fond adieu to these real life jezebels and pass the torch on to the next scholar, who hopefully will be able to fill in some of the remaining gaps in their remarkable life stories.[268]

The offshoot of all this is that Marie and Amelia are two of the most written about women of the war. When one considers that neither Marie nor Amelia was a major, or even a minor, contributor to the Civil War, the amount of words devoted to them is quite impressive and speaks volumes about the impression the two women made on people during their lifetimes.

# Notes

## INTRODUCTION

1. Undated address by Elizabeth Boatwright Coker, Elizabeth Boatwright Papers (henceforth referred to as EBC).

## CHAPTER 1

2. Ethel Battle to Elizabeth Boat Wright Coker, November 19, 1959, EBC; Battle to Coker, September 18, 1959, EBC; various, *Memorial*, 24; Carr family tree, Ancestry.com. Mrs. Battle was Amelia's granddaughter. The date comes from her family Bible. In an 1865 deposition, Amelia listed Philadelphia as her place of birth.
3. Snowden, *Countess Pourtales*, 18–19. This is a reprint of Selby's *A Checkered Life* with added material. While much of Selby's 1878 work is at best questionable and at worse slanderous (see Chapter Five), he did know Amelia personally, and his accounts of Amelia's and Marie's lives up to and including the Civil War years are considered mostly accurate.
4. Ibid., 19.
5. Various, *South Carolina Women*, 251; Gibbes, *Who Burnt Columbia?*, 20–21.
6. *Seventh Census*, 186b; *Eighth Census*, 28a.
7. Snowden, *Countess Pourtales*, 18; Holcomb, *Marriage*, 10; Ancestry.com.
8. Holcomb, *Marriage*, 10. Her wedding announcement to Peter Burton was published on January 21, 1841. One genealogist says Burton was born in 1820, but this goes against the numerous accounts that say that Burton was much older than Amelia.

9. Howe, *History*, 454. Reverend Dana was a graduate of Dartmouth, where his father, Dr. Daniel Davis, was president. Third Presbyterian was located at the corner of Archdale and West Streets in Charleston. The site is now a parking garage.
10. Coker, *La Belle*, 20; Snowden, *Countess Pourtales*, 19. Mrs. Coker copied the adoption papers verbatim in her novel.
11. Coker, *La Belle*, 48; *Eighth Census*, 28a; Massue, *Titled Nobility*, 1172. Nell S. Graydon, author of *Another Jezebel*, claims she saw the family Bible, but her date of 1842 for Marie's birth is too early. Marie's death notice in *Titled Nobility* conforms to 1850 being her birth year.
12. Snowden, *Countess Pourtales*, 21. I have chosen to use "Marie" because it is how she pronounced it and it is the most commonly used spelling of her name.
13. Ibid., 20; C.D.M., "A Fair Adventuress: Some Further Facts About the Countess Percele," *(Atlanta, GA) Constitution*, March 16, 1894, 4.
14. Notes of Miss Blanche Davidson on Amelia Boozer, EBC. Miss Davidson was a respected genealogist.
15. Howe, *History*, 711; Boozer, *Boozer Family*, 103; O'Neall, *Annals*, 22. Avaleigh got its name from an Irish church that the parents of one of the original church members attended. Reverend Hyde was at the church from 1845 to 1848. "Big Dave" is often confused with another David Boozer, who owned a large plantation in Newberry County at the same time. Contrary to several published accounts, Marie's stepfather was not a doctor.
16. O'Neall, *Annals*, 9–10, 92.
17. Boozer, *Boozer Family*, 103. Marie's adoption took place on July 17, 1850. Given that Amelia had four children from two marriages and Boozer had none from his two marriages, it is probable that Boozer was sterile.
18. Ibid., 169.
19. Ibid.; Snowden, *Countess Pourtales*, 21.
20. O'Neall, *Annals*, 169.
21. Coker, *La Belle*, 20–21; Snowden, *Countess Pourtales*, 21; Thomas H. Pope to Julian Bolick, August 22, 1957, EBC. Coker saw a copy of the will and copied it verbatim in *La Belle*. Selby claims that Marie was left $25,000; however, there is no mention of a lump cash sum in the will, so his figure may be the value of what Marie received.
22. Richardson, *Reports*, 22.
23. Ibid., 23–25.
24. Calcote, *Historical Sketches*, 2–3.
25. Newberry, Newberry County, South Carolina Genealogy Trails, Rosemont Cemetery Surname Index, genealogytrails.com; WKDK Road Trips, www.wkdk.com. I visited this site in 2013 and found the restaurant vacant and for sale.

26. Notes of Miss Blanche Davidson on Amelia Boozer, EBC.
27. Graydon, *Another Jezebel*, 64–65; Nell Graydon to Mr. Patterson,, October 1, 1959 Nell S. Graydon Papers (henceforth NSG-UNC). Though this is a work of fiction, Mrs. Graydon claimed in a letter that she had seen the records of the church hearing and included the actual charges in her novel.
28. Gilcreest, "Hugh Huger Toland," 263.
29. Ibid., 263–64.
30. Graydon, *Another Jezebel*, 65–66.
31. Snowden, *Countess Pourtales*, 21.
32. "Julian" to Coker, July 8, 1958, EBC; Notes of Miss Blanche Davidson on Amelia Boozer, EBC.
33. Notes of Miss Blanche Davidson on Amelia Boozer, EBC.
34. Snowden, *Countess Pourtales*, 21; Mitchell, Lena Norwood, "Jacob Norris Feaster and His Wife, Amelia Sees Boozer," undated unpublished manuscript, NSG-UNC.
35. Snowden, *Countess Pourtales*, 22; Mitchell, "Jacob Norris Feaster"; Gibbes, *Who Burnt Columbia?*, 20; Williams, *Old and New Columbia*, 118.
36. See Elmore, *Columbia Civil War Landmarks*, 11–15.
37. Williams, *Old and New Columbia*, 118; *Eighth Census*. Modern values calculated on Measuringworth.com.
38. Boozer, *Boozer Family*, 104; Jacob Jefferson Feaster, South Carolina Families, sc-families.org.
39. Untitled poem by Amelia Feaster, no date, EBC. The poem was probably written between 1857 and 1860.
40. See *Trinity Church* for more on the history of Trinity.

## CHAPTER 2

41. "Diary of Margaret Narcissa Feaster," 19–24.
42. Ibid., 50; Gibbes, *Who Burnt Columbia?*, 20; Woodward, *Mary Chesnut's Civil War*, 695.
43. *Indian River Advocate*, "Death of Mr. Jacob N. Feaster," January 25, 1895 118; Gibbes, *Who Burnt Columbia?*, 21; Williams, *Old and New Columbia*, 118.
44. Elmore, *Columbia Civil War Landmarks*, 11–15; various, *Memorial*, 24–25. Moore, *Columbia & Richland County*, 151–52; Williams, *Old and New Columbia*, 103. Freeze (1808–1892) returned to Columbia during Reconstruction as the sheriff of Richland County. Ironically, his son, Phineas Jr., served in the Confederate army.
45. Graydon, *Tales of Columbia*, 126; *Reports of the Committees of the Senate*, 83–84; Snowden, *Countess Pourtales*, 25.

46. Elmore, *Columbia Civil War Landmarks*, 31–32.
47. Woodward, *Mary Chesnut's Civil War*, 678; Elmore, *Columbia Civil War Landmarks*, 31–32.
48. Elmore, *Columbia Civil War Landmarks*, 33, 88; Williams, *Old and New Columbia*, 118. For more on Camp Sorghum and Camp Asylum, see Elmore, "Camp Sorghum."
49. *War of the Rebellion*, 8:160. Brigadier General John H. Winder was the controversial head of Confederate prisoner of war camps. He died from a heart attack while inspecting a prisoner of war camp in Florence, South Carolina, on February 7, 1865.
50. Gibbes, *Who Burnt Columbia?*, 21.
51. Sabre, *Nineteen Months*, 165, 169–70.
52. Ibid., 171.
53. Elmore, *Columbia Civil War Landmarks*, 14.
54. Ibid.; Joseph E. Johnston to William Mackall, January 26, 1865, William Whann Mackall Papers. By comparison, a Confederate private made eleven dollars a month.
55. Gibbes, *Who Burnt Columbia?*, 20.
56. Dickert, David Augustus, "The Countess Percele," *(Atlanta, GA) Constitution*, February 25, 1894, 5.
57. Snowden, *Countess Pourtales*, 51; various, *South Carolina Women*, 251; Letter to Coker from unknown addresser, August, 13, 1957, EBC; Wells, *Sketch*, 88–89; Dickert, "The Sorceress of the Congaree," *Newberry (SC) Herald & News*, Friday August 6, 1909; C.D.M. "Fair Adventuress." Selby claims that Marie's eyes were "gray-blue."
58. Woodward, *Mary Chesnut's Civil War*, 695; Lawrence, "Much Married," 23. The student body of South Carolina College was all male at the time.
59. Woodward, *Mary Chesnut's Civil War*, 695; Lawrence, "Much Married," 23; Williams, *Old and New Columbia*, 118.
60. Snowden, *Countess Pourtales*, 23, 8.
61. Ibid., 8; Dickert, "Sorceress"; Letter to Coker from unknown addresser, August, 13, 1957, EBC; C.D.M., "Fair Adventuress," 4.
62. Graydon, *Tales of Columbia*, 35–36; Moore, *Columbia & Richland County*, 112.
63. *Catalogue of the Officers and Pupils*, 11–12.
64. Uray and Bernardin, *History*, 9. In the 1860s, the Mother Superior of the school was Sister Mary Baptista, née Lynch, the sister of Bishop Patrick Lynch of the Diocese of Charleston. In 1863, the two schools discussed a merger, with the convent moving to the Barhamville campus, but nothing came of those negotiations.
65. *Metropolitan Catholic Almanac*, 356.
66. Lawrence, "Much Married," 23; C.D.M., "Fair Adventuress," 4.

67. "Diary of Margaret Narcissa Feaster," 19–24; Dickert, "Countess Percele"; C.D.M., "Fair Adventuress," 4. "Upper tendom" was a nineteenth-century term that referred to the very wealthy. Gary (1831–1881) was a graduate of Harvard and was a successful lawyer and legislator before the Civil War. Gary commanded the last Confederate troops out of Richmond and helped escort Jefferson Davis and the Confederate Cabinet south. In 1876, he cofounded the still controversial "Red Shirt" movement, which led to the end of Reconstruction in South Carolina.
68. Woodward, *Mary Chestnut's Civil War*, 695; Ancestry.com; *Journal of the Congress*, 303.
69. Graydon, *Tales of Columbia*, 126; Woodward, *Mary Chestnut's Civil War*, 695. In *La Belle*, Coker claims that Amelia stole the items to prevent the marriage because she saw Willie as a pauper. Mrs. Graydon, however, does not mention Willie in *Another Jezebel*.
70. Graydon, *Tales of Columbia*, 126. Information on Capers's postwar life is from Ancestry.com.
71. Ibid.; Snowden, *Countess Pourtales*, 5. Mrs. Graydon is the only source for Marie's infatuation with Preston, which she included in *Another Jezebel*. Mrs. Coker makes no mention of it in any of her writings or in her papers.
72. Graydon, *Tales of Columbia*, 126–27; Lawrence, "Much Married," 23.
73. Graydon, *Tales, of Columbia*, 126; Lawrence, "Much Married," 23; Woodward, *Mary Chestnut's Civil War*, 695.
74. Lawrence, "Much Married," 23, Snowden, *Countess Pourtales*, 24–25; Wells, *Sketch*, 89.
75. Jones, "Guard at Andersonville," 5.
76. Ibid.
77. "Diary of Margaret Narcissa Feaster," 69.
78. Simms, *City Laid Waste*, 68, 83. See Elmore, *Carnival of Destruction* for more about the burning of Columbia.
79. Sabre, *Nineteen Months*, 173.
80. Sherman, *Memoirs*, 280–81, 286; Gibbes, *Who Burnt Columbia?*, 21.
81. *Columbia (SC) Phoenix*, March 23, 1865, 4; Gibbes, *Who Burnt Columbia?*, 21; Sherman, *Memoirs*, 295.
82. Sabre, *Nineteen Months*, 173.
83. Woodward, *Mary Chestnut's Civil War*, 753.
84. Various, *South Carolina Women*, 253.
85. Ibid., 259.
86. Snowden, *Countess Pourtales*, 6–7. Selby is the creator of this rumor, which is explored in Chapter Five. Kilpatrick was one of the war's biggest womanizers. Television journalist Anderson Cooper is a direct descendant of General Kilpatrick.
87. Ibid., 28.

88. Ibid., 295; *War of the Rebellion*, 47:1, 23. The boat arrived on March 14, 1865.
89. Lawrence, "Much Married," 23.
90. Ibid.

## CHAPTER 3

91. Various, *Memorial*, 20–21.
92. Ibid.
93. *Journal of the House*, 138, 222.
94. Graydon, *Another Jezebel*, 214. Howard commanded the Army of the Tennessee during the Campaign of the Carolinas and was Sherman's second in command.
95. Snowden, *Countess Pourtales*, 28–30, Gibbes, *Who Burnt Columbia?*, 21, Bellows, *Historical Sketch*; E-mail from Kent Book, librarian, Union League of New York, to Tom Elmore, June 25, 2013. In 1866, the club did bring some Southern loyalists who were attending a convention to New York from Philadelphia.
96. *State*, "Mrs. Coker Gives Witty Account of Research for Recent Book," November 3, 1959, 8A. That person was G.W. Blunt White, who is listed at the end of the bibliography of *La Belle*.
97. Coker, *La Belle*, 217–18.
98. Mitchell, "Mrs. Wilson Passes Away," *East Coast Advocate*, August 10, 1917.
99. Gibbes, *Who Burnt Columbia?*, 21.
100. Jacob Jefferson Feaster, South Carolina Families, sc-families.org.
101. Coker, *La Belle*, 217.
102. *Journal of the Senate*, 573; "The Ohio Icicle," John Sherman (1823–1900), first went to Washington in 1854 as a Republican congressman from Ohio. He was appointed to the U.S. Senate in 1861 and served there until being named U.S. Treasury secretary in 1877.

  He returned to the Senate in 1881 and wrote one of the most important pieces of legislation ever passed by Congress, the Sherman Anti-Trust Act of 1890, which still to this day puts limits on monopolies, trusts and market manipulations. Senator Sherman remained in the Senate until 1897, when President William McKinley named him secretary of state as a reward for his years of service to the Republican Party. Ironically, John had helped write the Pendleton Civil Service Reform Act of 1883, which stated that federal government jobs should be awarded on merit rather than political patronage and favoritism. He stayed in that post for one year before retiring from politics.

103. See Thorndike, *Sherman Letters*. During this period, the general spent most of his time at his headquarters in St. Louis, while the senator was mainly in Washington.
104. Ibid., 609; Library of Congress, A Century of Lawmaking for a New Nation: U.S. Congressional Documents and Debates, 1774–1875, memory.loc.gov.
105. *Reports of the Committees of the Senate*, 83.
106. Ibid.
107. Ibid.
108. Ibid.
109. Ibid., 83–84.
110. Ibid., 84.
111. Ibid., 84–85. A sutler was a civilian contracted by the military to sell dry and sundry goods, canned food and whiskey to soldiers in the field. The term "sutler" dates from at least the eighteenth century and is believed to have come from the Dutch word *soetelaar* or *zoetelaar*, which means "one who does dirty work." Sutlers, as rule, had a reputation for being unscrupulous price gougers.
112. Ibid.
113. Ibid., 85. The generals referred to here are Lieutenant General Ulysses S. Grant, commanding general, U.S. Army; Major General Oliver Otis Howard; Major General George Terry, commander of the X$^{th}$ Corps, who captured Fort Fisher outside Wilmington, North Carolina, in January 1864; Major General Justin Kilpatrick, Sherman's chief of cavalry; and Major General Edmund Schriver. The last name listed, Edmund Schriver, is a bit odd, as his postings would have made it impossible for him to have met Amelia during the war.
114. *Journal of the Senate*, 671; *Journal of the House of Representatives of the United States, Being the First Session*, 94, 1040, 1113; *Journal of the House of Representatives of the United State, Being the Second Session*, 94. South Carolina's two Senate seats were vacant at this time.
115. *Journal of the House of Representatives of the United State, Being the Second Session*, 1113; Williams, *Biographical Encyclopedia*, 36.
116. Letter from Captain Emlen Carpenter to Mrs. Feaster, n.d., Carpenter Family Papers. I am grateful to historian Eric Wittenberg for sharing this letter with me.
117. Ibid.
118. Gibbes, *Who Burnt Columbia?*, 21; Snowden, *Countess Pourtales*, 30; Dickert, "Sorceress"; Dickert, false obituary, *Augusta (GA) Chronicle*, September 18, 1927.
119. Snowden, *Countess Pourtales*, 31, 54.
120. Coker, *La Belle*, 220.

121. *New York Times*, Obituary notices, June 13, 1894.
122. *Documents of the Board of Councilmen*, 138. Zouaves were infantry units whose uniforms were based on North African designs that often included fezzes and turbans for headgear and bright colors, which made them popular for pre–Civil War parades and gatherings but also made them stand out on the battlefield. Zouaves were not all show, as they were also known for their unique drilling and fighting style and were viewed as elite troops. There were Zouave units in both the Confederate and Union armies during the Civil War.
123. *New York Times*, "Local Business Troubles," March 14, 1883; *Trow's New York City Director*, 100; *New York Times*, "Ives, Beecher & Co. Schedule," April 11, 1883. Some accounts state that Beecher also imported oil. Selby claims that Beecher was a member of the Union League, but there is no record of this.
124. Snowden, *Countess Pourtales*, 31, 54; Coker, *La Belle*, 225–30, 237. Selby states that they were married in an Episcopal church in Audubon Park, Washington Heights. However, the Church of the Intercession, which fits that description, was not in use until 1872. Coker puts their marriage date in *La Belle* as Christmas Day 1865, while Selby argues for 1866. The latter date is the most commonly accepted.
125. Coker, Elizabeth Boatwright [Elizabeth Old Girl, pseud.], "Sandal or Scandal: Being the True Story of the Countess Pourtales, Formerly Miss Marie Boozer of Columbia S.C.," unpublished manuscript, EBC, 31–32, 53.
126. Leonard, *Who's Who*, 105; Marie de Pourtalès to Ethland Feaster, March 18, 1884, EBC; Snowden, *Countess Pourtales*, 32; Coker, "Sandal," EBC, 22.
127. Leonard, *Who's Who*, 1041. The Naval Academy Sailing Squadron annually awards the Lloyd Phoenix Cup to the winner of its yachting race. Mrs. Coker claimed that White had materials on Phoenix as well.
128. Snowden, *Countess Pourtales*, 19; Coker, "Sandal," EBC, 21; Coker, *La Belle*, 278. Selby claims that Marie shot Phoenix, but there is no evidence to support his claim. He also claimed that the Beecher marriage lasted only two years. I have been unable to locate any documentation regarding their divorce.
129. Marie de Pourtalès to Ethland Feaster, March 18, 1884, EBC; Wells, *Sketch*, 89; *New York Sun*, "Lloyd Phoenix Dead," April 1, 1926, 23.
130. *Annual Register*, 78; Hamersly, Leonard and Holmes, *Who's Who*, 100. It is unclear if Preston earned a medical degree, as the only reference to him as a doctor is in his obituary.
131. *New York Times*, "Ives, Beecher & Co. Schedule," April 11, 1883.

132. Ethel Battle to Elizabeth Boatwright Coker, November 19, 1959, EBC; New York State Education Department; Pennsylvania Church and Town Records; Snowden, *Countess Pourtales*, 48. The 1860 U.S. census shows only one man named Bostwick living in Columbia in 1860, a nineteen-year-old mulatto carpenter.
133. *Indian River Advocate*, "Death of Mr. Jacob N. Feaster," January 25, 1895; Jacob Jefferson Feaster, South Carolina Families, sc-families.org. Jacob Jr. does not appear in any records after the 1870 U.S. census.

# CHAPTER 4

134. Mitchell, "Mrs. Wilson Passes Away," *East Coast Advocate*, August 10, 1917; Gibbes, *Who Burnt Columbia?*, 21; Coker, "Sandal," EBC, 35; *Washington Post*, June 6, 1905, 6.
135. Gibbes, *Who Burnt Columbia?*, 21; Coker, "Sandal," EBC, 35; Biographical information from Ancestry.com and Geneanet.org; Akeley, Mrs. O.E., "The Social World," *(NY) Globe and Commercial Advertiser*, February 29, 1904, 4; *Washington Post*, June 6, 1905, 6. Some accounts incorrectly state that the count was younger than Marie.
136. Biographical information from Ancestry.com, gw.Geneanet.org and *Washington Post*, June 6, 1905, 6.
137. *Washington Post*, June 6, 1905, 6. Information on Holladay from Wikipedia.com.
138. *New York Times*, February 10, 1876, 2; *Washington Post*, June 6, 1905, 6.
139. *Chicago Tribune*, August 27, 1898; *San Francisco Chronicle*, "An Ungrateful Son-In-Law," January 6, 1876. At the time of Jenny's death, the count was assigned to Washington.
140. *San Francisco Chronicle*, "An Ungrateful Son-in-Law."
141. Ibid.
142. Ibid.
143. Ibid.
144. C.D.M., "Fair Adventuress."
145. Wikipedia.com articles "Diocese of Baltimore" and "James Roosevelt Bayley." Bayley served as Baltimore's archbishop from 1872 until his death in 1877.
146. Massue, *Titled Nobility*, 1172; *State*, "Heroine of Mrs. Graydon's Book Writes of Her Travels Abroad During the 1800's [sic]," February 23, 1960, B6.
147. *State*, "Heroine."
148. Ibid.

149. Marie de Pourtalès to unknown party, no date, NSG-UNC.
150. Ancestry.com; *State*, "Heroine."
151. *State*, "Heroine"; C.D.M., "Fair Adventuress."
152. *State*, "Heroine"; *Washington Post*, June 6, 1905, 6.
153. Simkins and Patton, *Women of the Confederacy*, 271; *Chicago Tribune*, August 27, 1898.
154. Winchester, *Krakotoa*, 138–42. Additional information from Wikipedia articles on Jakarta and Bogor.
155. *State*, "Heroine."
156. Ibid.
157. Ibid.
158. Ibid.
159. Winchester, Simon, *Krakotoa*, 264, 240–41. Some believe that the death toll could have been as high as 120,000.
160. Ibid., 283, 291. Some believe the particles could have gone even higher, up to thirty miles in the air. A new volcanic island, Anak Krakatau (Child of Krakatoa) broke water in the same spot in 1930 and is still growing. It had a major eruption in 2012, and some believe it could be even deadlier than Krakatoa.
161. *State*, "Heroine."
162. Ibid.
163. Countess de Pourtalès to Ethland Feaster, March 18, 1884, EBC.
164. *Chicago Tribune*, August 27, 1898.
165. Ibid.
166. Baring, *Puppet Show*, 193–94.
167. Countess de Pourtalès to Ethland Feaster, n.d., NSG-UNC.
168. Countess de Pourtalès to unknown, n.d., NSG-UNC.
169. Coker, *La Belle*, 48; *State*, "Heroine"; NSG-UNC.
170. *State*, "Heroine"; Ancestry.com.
171. Coker, *La Belle*, 48.
172. Geneat, geneanet.org; Letter from Countess de Pourtales, no date, NSG-UNC.
173. Battle to Coker, EBC; *East Coast Advocate*, August 10, 1917; *Indian River Chronicle*, August 10, 1917.
174. Ancestry.com; Coker, *La Belle*, 48.
175. Register of the Department of State, 57.
. Leonard, *Who's Who*, 100; Coker, *La Belle*, 48.
176. Parker, *Powell Papers*, 326. The younger Beecher's writings appeared in the August 1910 issue of *Harper's* magazine, the February 16, 1888 issue of the *Nation* and the September 20, 1902 issue of the *Saturday Review*.
177. U.S. Passport Applications; Ancestry.com.; "Obituary," *Alumni Hoare* 20, no. 2 (Summer 1940), 85; Political Graveyard, politicalgraveyard.com/bio/

beechem-beesley.html#334.68.19. The wedding date is conjecture, based on the fact that Preston makes no mention of a wife in a December 1914 passport application but mentions one in a February 1915 passport application.
178. Julia C. Feaster Fields, www.findagrave.com.
179. *State*, "Heroine."

## CHAPTER 5

180. Sherman, *Memoirs*, 295.
181. Selby, *Checkered Life*; Anderson, *Two Scholarly Friends*, 355n47.
182. Coker, *La Belle*, 47.
183. Information on Cora Pearl from Wikipedia.org.
184. Coker, "Sandal," EBC, 8.
185. Graydon, *Another Jezebel*, 218.
186. Coker, *La Belle*, 313–14; Coker, "Sandal," EBC, 26.
187. Selby, *Memorabilia*.
188. Anderson, *Two Scholarly Friends*, 83; Gergel, *Faithful Index*, 101. A dorm was later named for the professor.
189. Snowden, *Countess Pourtales*, 6–7.
190. Ibid., 7, 9.
191. Anderson, *Two Scholarly Friends*, 85. John Bennett (1865–1956) was a northern transplant to Charleston, South Carolina. He is best known for his decade-long work in studying the area's Gullah language and culture, culminated in his 1946 book, *The Doctor and the Dead*. James Gadsen Holmes (1881–1942) was a successful Columbian and Charleston merchant. "Young Selby" refers to Gilbert A. Selby (1868–1955), son of Julian Selby, a successful printer and writer in his own right.
192. Ibid., 86.
193. Ibid., 83.
194. Ibid., 180. Cooker identified Snowden as "Felix Old Boy" in her bibliography of *La Belle*, but it seems to have been common knowledge long before then.
195. Scott, *Random Recollections*.
196. Wells, *Sketch*, 88.
197. Ibid., 88–89.
198. *Anderson (S.C.) Intelligence*, November 6, 1884; *Daily Morning Astorian*, July 19, 1885.
199. *Daily Morning Astorian*, July 19, 1885.
200. Dickert, "Countess Percele," 5; New Berry County Obituaries, South Carolina Genealogy Trails, genealogytrails.com; Wyckoff, David Augustus Dickert, pittmans.tripod.com/dickert.html.

201. Dickert, "Countess Percele"; Faust, *Historical Times*, 177, 547–48.
202. Dickert, "Countess Percele."
203. Coker to Naomi Burton, n.d., EBC.
204. C.D.M., "Fair Adventuress," 4.
205. Ibid.
206. Anonymous, "Six Adventuresses, Women Who by Beauty or Wit Ensnared and Fleeced Notable Men," *St. Paul (MN) Daily Globe*, September 9, 1894. The article may have originally been published in the *New York Recorder*.
207. Ibid.
208. Ibid. The bad pun was presumably intended.
209. *Chicago Tribune*, August 27, 1898.
210. Gibbes, *Who Burnt Columbia?*, 21–22.
211. Various, *South Carolina Women*, 251, 253, 259.
212. Chesnut, *Diary*.
213. Chesnut, *Diary*, edited by Ben Ames Williams, 466, 502. This version was reprinted with a new forward in 1980 by Harvard University Press.
214. Woodward, *Mary Chesnut's Civil War*, 695, 753–54; Woodward and Muhlenfeld, *Private Mary Chesnut*.
215. *Washington Post*, June 6, 1905.
216. *Jasper (IN) Weekly Courier*, August 10, 1906, 2. This feature also ran in newspapers in Louisiana, Missouri, Nebraska and Utah. Efforts to obtain information on "Terison" have been unsuccessful. It should be noted that several accounts make references to stories about Marie from English newspapers, but I can neither confirm nor deny this.
217. Ibid.
218. Ibid.
219. Coker to Burton, n.d., EBC; Dickert, "Sorceress," 1; New Berry County Obituaries, South Carolina Genealogy Trails, genealogytrails.com; Wyckoff, David Augustus Dickert pittmans.tripod.com/dickert.html.
220. Simkins and Patton, *Women of the Confederacy*, 271; Dickert, "Countess Perceles."
221. Lawrence, "Much Married," 23. The United Confederate Veterans (UCV) existed from 1889 until 1951 and was similar in nature to today's American Legion and Veterans of Foreign Wars. The still active Sons of Confederate Veterans, founded in 1896, is an offshoot of the UCV.
222. Ibid.
223. Ibid.
224. Ibid.
225. Williams, *Old and New Columbia*, 118. Williams was born in 1850.
226. Simkins and Patton, *Women of the Confederacy*, 63, 271.
227. Various, *South Carolina*, 312.

228. Ibid.
229. Barrett, *Sherman's March*, 93, 97, 128, 136, 308.
230. Turner Classic Movies, www.tcm.com/tcmdb/title/673/Jezebel; Webster, *American Dictionary*, retrieved at 1828.mshaffer.com/d/jezebel. The original nineteenth-century definition used the now obsolete word "vitious." There is little similarity between the play/film (both of which are set in New Orleans) and the lives of Amelia and Marie other than that the leading female character is a strong-willed woman who will stop at nothing to get her way. Davis won the Oscar for best actress for her portrayal of the title character, which legend says was a consolation prize for not being cast as Scarlett O'Hara in *Gone with the Wind*.
231. Epps, *Literary South Carolina*, 72.
232. Graydon, *Another Jezebel*; Graydon to Patterson, NSG-UNC.
233. *State*, December 7, 1958, found in Nell S. Graydon Papers, Manuscript Collection, South Caroliniana Library, University of South Carolina, Columbia (hereafter NSG-USC).
234. Epps, *Literary South Carolina*, 60.
235. Ibid., 60–61; Boatwright Genealogy, Elizabeth Moore Boatwright Coker, boatwrightgenealogy.com/ElizabethMBoatwrightCoker.html.
236. Coker, *La Belle*, 8.
237. Ibid.
238. Coker to Burton, n.d., EBC; Graydon to Coker, November 7, 1959, EBC. Mrs. Graydon still has not shared her research, as very little of it can be found at either her papers at the University of South Carolina or those at the University of North Carolina.
239. Coker to Ethel Battle, October 10, 1959, EBC.
240. *La Belle*, 313–315.
241. Ibid., 315.
242. Copies of reviews in EBC.
243. *State*, "Living Descendant's Letter Sheds Light," November 1, 1959, D4.
244. Graydon to Coker, November 7, 1959, EBC. Mrs. Graydon donated royalties from the book to the South Caroliniana Library at the University of South Carolina.
245. Battle to Coker, November 6, 1959, November 3, 1959, February 3, 1960, EBC.
246. Battle to Coker, November 3, 1959, EBC.
247. *State*, "Living Descendant's Letter"; *State*, "Heroine." Ironically, Mrs. Coker had planned on doing the same thing, but Mrs. Graydon beat her to it.
248. Battle to Coker, February 3, 1960, EBC; Scott Bartlett to Coker, February 3, 1960, EBC; Battle to Coker, February 6, 1959, EBC.
249. Graydon, *Tales of Columbia*, 125–27.

250. Coker, "Sandal," EBC.
251. Ibid.
252. Coker, *La Belle*, 47.
253. Ibid.
254. Ibid., 46.
255. Ibid.
256. Ibid., 48.
257. Ibid.
258. Jones, "Guard at Andersonville."
259. Ibid.
260. Boozer, *Boozer Family*.
261. Davis, *Sherman's March*, 154–55, 180, 186, 194–95, 201, 211–14, 219.
262. Royster, *Destructive War*, 32.
263. Moore, *Columbia & Richland County*, 204.
264. Martin, *Kill-Cavalry*, 217–18, 221–23, 226. In a conversation with me, Martin admitted that he was wrong about Marie's fate.
265. Elmore, "Lurid Legends," 42–47.
266. Southeast Archeology Center: The Battle of Monroe's Crossroads, www.nps.gov/seac/research/fp/fp00007/fp00007.htm; Belew and Scott, *Cavalry Clash*, 31, 38, 56.
267. Wittenberg, *Battle of Monroe's Crossroads*, 252–54.
268. Elmore, *Carnival of Destruction*, 273; Elmore, *Columbia Civil War Landmarks*, 44–45.

# Bibliography

## PRIMARY SOURCES

Anderson, Mary Crow, ed. *Two Scholarly Friends: Yates Snowden–John Bennett Correspondence, 1902–1932*. Columbia: University of South Carolina Press, 1993.

Baring, Maurice. *The Puppet Show of Memory*. London: William Heineman, 1922.

Chesnut, Mary Boykin Miller. *A Diary from Dixie*. New York: D. Appleton and Company, 1905.

———. *A Diary from Dixie*. Edited by Ben Ames Williams. New York: Houghton Mifflin Co., 1949. Reprint, Boston: Harvard University Press, 1980.

Coker, Elizabeth Boatwright. "La Belle Marie: The Final Chapter." *Sandlapper: The Magazine of South Carolina* 9, no. 11 (November 1976).

Gibbes, Colonel James G. *Who Burnt Columbia?* Newberry, SC: Elbert H. Aull Company, 1902.

Holcomb, Brent Howard, ed. *Marriage and Death Notices from Columbia, South Carolina, Newspapers, 1838–1860*. Greenville, SC: Southern Historical Press, 1982.

Jones, James Dunwoody. "A Guard at Andersonville." *Civil War Times Illustrated* 3 (1964). Reprinted in *Andersonville*. N.p.: Eastern Acorn Press, 1989.

Lawrence, Robert de Treville. "The Much Married Miss Mary Boozer." *Confederate Veteran* 24, no. 1 (January 1921).

O'Neall, John Belton, LLD. *The Annals of Newberry*. Charleston, SC: S.G. Courtenay and Company, 1859.

# Bibliography

Sabre, Gilbert E. *Nineteen Months a Prisoner of War*. New York: American News Company, 1865.

Scott, Edwin J., *Random Recollections of a Long Life: 1806–1876*. Columbia, SC: Charles A. Calvo Jr. Printer, 1884.

Selby, Julian A. *Memorabilia and Anecdotal Reminiscences of Columbia S.C. and Incidents Connected Therewith*. Columbia, SC: R.L. Bryan Company, 1905.

Sherman, William T. *Memoirs of General William T. Sherman*. Vol. 2. New York: D. Appleton and Company, 1875.

Simms, William Gilmore. *A City Laid Waste: The Capture, Sack and Destruction of the City of Columbia*. Columbia: University of South Carolina Press, 2005.

Thorndike, Rachel Sherman, ed. *The Sherman Letters: Correspondence Between General and Senator Sherman from 1837–1891*. New York: Charles Scribner's Sons, 1894.

Various. *South Carolina Women in the Confederacy: Records Collected by the Committee from South Carolina State Division United Daughters of the Confederacy*. Edited by State Committee UDC. Columbia SC: State Co., 1903.

Williams, James Franklin. *Old and New Columbia*. Columbia, SC: Epworth Orphanage Press, 1929.

Woodward, C. Vann, and Elisabeth Muhlenfeld, eds. *The Private Mary Chesnut: The Unpublished Civil War Diaries*. New York: Oxford University Press, 1984.

Woodward, C. Vann, ed. *Mary Chesnut's Civil War*. New Haven, CT: Yale University Press, 1981.

## OFFICIAL PUBLICATIONS

*Alumni Hoare* 20, no. 2 (Summer 1940). Alumni publication of St. Paul's School, Concord, NH.

*Annual Register of the Officers and Students of Columbia College*. Register of Columbia College, New York, 1884.

*Catalogue of the Officers and Pupils of the S.C. Female Institute at Barhamville, Near Columbia: Under the Direction of Dr. E. Marks and Rev. W.H. Tyler; During the First Session of the Academic Year 1840–1841*. Columbia SC: J.C. Morgan, 1841.

*The Columbia Directory, Containing the Names, Business and Residence of the Inhabitants*. Columbia, SC: Julian Selby, 1859.

*Documents of the Board of Councilmen of the City of New York*. Vol. 2, part 2. New York: McSpedon & Baker, Printers to the Common Council, n.d.

*Eighth Census of the United States 1860*. South Carolina, Richland, Sumter and Union Districts.

*Journal of the Congress of the Confederate States of America 1861–1865*. Vol. 4. Washington, D.C.: Government Printing Office, 1904.

*Journal of the House of Representatives of the United States, Being the First Session of the Thirty-Ninth Congress*. Washington, D.C.: Government Printing Office, 1865.

# Bibliography

*Journal of the House of Representatives of the United States, Being the Second Session of the Thirty-Ninth Congress.* Washington, D.C.: Government Printing Office, 1867.

*Journal of the Senate of the United States of America, Being the First Session of the Thirty-Ninth Congress.* Washington, D.C.: Government Printing Office, 1865.

Massue, Melville Henry. *The Titled Nobility of Europe: An International Peerage; or, "Who's Who," of the Sovereigns, Princes, and Nobles of Europe.* London: Harrison & Sons, 1914.

*The Metropolitan Catholic Almanac, and Laity's Directory for the United States.* Baltimore, MD: John Murphy & Company, 1860.

New York State Education Department. Office of Cultural Education, Albany, NY. *U.S. Census Mortality Schedules, New York, 1858–1880.* Archive roll number M7, census year 1870, census location: New York, NY, Line 21. Found on Ancestry.com.

Pennsylvania Church and Town Records, 1708–1985. Provo UT: Ancestry.com Operations, Inc., 2011.

Register of the Department of State, November 10, 1913. Washington, D.C.: Government Printing Office, 1913.

*The Reports of the Committees of the Senate of the United States for the First Session Thirty-Ninth Congress, 1865–1866.* Washington, D.C.: Government Printing Office, 1866.

Richardson, J.S.G., state reporter. *Reports of Cases in Equity Argued and Demanded in the Court of Appeals and Court of Errors of South Carolina.* Vol. 4. Columbia, SC: R.W. Gibbes, 1853.

*Seventh Census of the United States 1850.* South Carolina, Newberry District.

*Trow's New York City Director.* Vol. 90. New York: Trow City Directory Company, 1876.

U.S. Passport Applications, January 2, 1906–March 31, 1925. National Archives and Records Administration (NARA), Collection Number: ARC Identifier 583830/MLR Number A1 534; NARA Series: M1490; Roll: 234. Washington D.C.

Various. *Memorial, Testimony and Letters of Federal Prisoners on the Claim of P.F. Frazee, a Loyal Citizen of New Jersey, for Property Destroyed at Columbia, S.C. February 17, 1865 by the Forces of Maj. Gen. Sherman.* Washington, D.C.: McGill, Witherow, Printers and Stereotypers, 1866.

———. *South Carolina: The WPA Guide to the Palmetto State.* New York: Oxford University Press, 1941.

*War of the Rebellion: A Compilation of the Official Records of the Union and Confederate Armies.* 128 vols. Washington, D.C.: Government Printing Office, 1880–1901.

# Bibliography

## NEWSPAPERS

*Anderson Intelligence*, Anderson, S.C.
*Chicago Tribune*, Chicago, IL.
*Columbia Phoenix*, Columbia, SC.
*Constitution*, Atlanta, GA.
*Daily Morning Astorian*, Astoria, OR.
*East Coast Advocate*, Titusville, FL.
*Globe and Commercial Advertiser*, New York, NY.
*Indian River Advocate*, Titusville, FL.
*Jasper Weekly Courier*, Jasper, IN.
*Newberry Herald & News*, Newberry, SC.
*New York Sun*, New York, NY.
*New York Times*, New York, NY.
*State*, Columbia, SC.
*Washington Post*, Washington, D.C.

## MANUSCRIPTS

Carpenter Family Papers. Historical Society of Pennsylvania, Philadelphia.
"The Diary of Margaret Narcissa Feaster, 1860–1865." Manuscript Collection, South Caroliniana Library, University of South Carolina, Columbia.
Elizabeth Boatwright Coker Papers. Manuscript Collection, South Caroliniana Library, University of South Carolina, Columbia.
Nell S. Graydon Papers, #3446-z. Southern Historical Collection, Wilson Library, University of North Carolina, Chapel Hill.
Nell S. Graydon Papers. Manuscript Collection, South Caroliniana Library, University of South Carolina, Columbia.
William Whann Mackall Papers, #1299. Southern Historical Collection, Wilson Library, University of North Carolina, Chapel Hill.

## SECONDARY SOURCES

Barrett, John G., *Sherman's March Through the Carolinas*. Chapel Hill: University of North Carolina Press, 1956.
Belew, Kenneth, and Douglas D. Scott. *Cavalry Clash in the Sandhills: The Battle of Monroe's Crossroads North Carolina 10 March, 1865*. N.p.: U.S. Department of the Interior, National Park Service, Midwest Archeological Center, Southeast Archeological Center and the University of Wisconsin–Madison, 1997.

# Bibliography

Bellows, Henry W. *Historical Sketch of the Union League Club of New York: Its Origin, Organization and Work 1863–1879.* New York: G.P. Putnam's Sons, 1879.

Boozer, Mary Elizabeth, *The Boozer Family of South Carolina.* Columbia, SC: R.L. Bryan Company, 1970.

Calcote, Reverend Claude A. *Historical Sketches of Aveleigh Presbyterian Church, Newberry, S.C* Newberry, SC: Herald & News, 1935.

Coker, Elizabeth Boatwright. *La Belle: A Novel Based on the Life of the Notorious Southern Belle, Marie Boozer.* New York: E.P. Dutton & Co., Inc., 1959.

Davis, Burke. *Sherman's March.* New York: Vintage Books, 1988.

Elmore, Tom. "Camp Sorghum." *Columbia Metropolitan* (September/October 2005).

———. *A Carnival of Destruction: Sherman's Invasion of South Carolina.* Charleston, SC: Jogglingboard Press, 2012.

———. *Columbia Civil War Landmarks.* Charleston, SC: The History Press, 2011.

———. "Lurid Legends of a Wayward Woman." *Civil War* (August 1997).

Epps, Edwin C. *Literary South Carolina.* Spartanburg, SC: Hub City Writers Project, 2004.

Faust, Patricia L., ed. *Historical Times Illustrated Encyclopedia of the Civil War.* New York: Harper Perennial, 1991.

Gergel, Pat, ed. *Faithful Index: The University of South Carolina Campus; A Guide to Buildings and People.* Columbia: University of South Carolina Office of Information Services, 1976.

Gilcreest, Edgar Lorrington, MD. "Hugh Huger Toland: Part I." *California and Western Medicine* 48, no. 4 (April 1938).

Graydon, Nell S. *Another Jezebel: A Yankee Spy in South Carolina.* Columbia, SC: R.L. Bryan Company, 1958.

———. *Tales of Columbia.* Columbia, SC: R.L. Bryan Company, 1964.

Hamersly, Lewis Randolph, John William Leonard and Frank R. Holmes. *Who's Who in New York City and State.* New York: L.R. Hamersly Company, 1909.

Howe, George. *History of the Presbyterian Church in South Carolina.* Vol. 2. Columbia, SC: Duffie & Chapman, 1883.

Leonard, John W., ed. *Who's Who in New York City and State: A Biographical Dictionary of Contemporaries.* 4th ed. New York: L.R. Hamersly & Company, 1909.

Martin, Samuel J. *Kill-Cavalry: The Life of Union General Hugh Judson Kilpatrick.* Madison, NJ: Farleigh Dickinson University Press, 1996.

Moore, John Hammond. *Columbia & Richland County: A South Carolina Community, 1740–1990.* Columbia: University of South Carolina Press, 1993.

Parker, Hershel. *The Powell Papers: A Confidence Man Amok Among the Anglo-American Literati.* Evanston, IL: Northwestern University Press, 2011.

Royster, Charles. *The Destructive War.* New York: Alfred A. Knopf, 1991.

# Bibliography

Selby, Julian [One Who Knows, pseud.]. *A Checkered Life: Being A Brief History of the Countess Pourtales, Formerly Miss Marie Boozer of Columbia S.C.* Columbia, SC: Printed at the office of the *Daily Phoenix*, 1878.

Simkins, Francis Butler, and James Welch Patton. *The Women of the Confederacy.* New York: Garrett and Massie, Inc., 1936.

Snowden, Yates [Felix Old Boy, pseud.]. *The Countess Pourtales.* Columbia, SC: S&H Publishing Co., 1915.

*Trinity Church, Columbia S.C.: One Hundred and Twenty-Fifth Anniversary 1937.* Columbia, SC: State Company, 1937.

Uray, Richard M., and Elizabeth D. Bernardin, eds. *A History of St. Peter's Church.* Columbia, SC: St. Peter's Parrish, 1990.

Webster, Noah, *American Dictionary of English Language.* New Haven, CT: Hezekiah Howe, 1828.

Williams, H. Clay. *Biographical Encyclopedia of Massachusetts of the Nineteenth Century.* Vol. 2. Boston: Metropolitan Publishing and Engraving Company, 1883.

Winchester, Simon. *Krakotoa: The Day the World Exploded; August 27, 1883.* New York: Harper Collins Publishers, 2003.

Wittenberg, Eric J. *The Battle of Monroe's Crossroads and the Civil War's Final Campaign.* New York: Savas Beatie LLC, 2006.

## WEBSITES

Ancestry.com. www.Ancestry.com.
Boatwright Genealogy. boatwrightgenealogy.com/ElizabethMBoatwrightCoker.html.
Find-a-Grave. www.findagrave.com.
Genealogy Trails. genealogytrails.com.
Geneanet. geneanet.org.
Library of Congress. memory.loc.gov.
Measuringworth. Measuringworth.com.
National Park Service. www.nps.gov/seac/research/fp/fp00007/fp00007.htm.
The Political Grave Yard. politicalgraveyard.com.
South Carolina Families. sc-families.org/tree/I745.html.
Southeast Archeology Center: The Battle of Monroe's Crossroads. www.nps.gov/seac/research/fp/fp00007/fp00007.htm.
Turner Classic Movies. www.tcm.com.
Wikipedia. Wikipedia.com.
WKDK, Newberry, SC. www.wkdk.com.
Wyckoff, Max. David Augustus Dickert. pittmans.tripod.com/dickert.html.

# *Index*

## A

*A Checkered Life*  65, 68, 69
*Another Jezebel*  68, 77, 79, 81, 84
Astor House Hotel  44
Avaleigh Presbyterian Church  17

## B

Baltimore, Maryland  57
Baring, Maurice  61, 86
Barrett, Dr. John G.  77
Batavia, Java  59, 60, 61
Battle, Elizabeth  84
Beecher, John S.  52, 56
Beecher, Preston  53
Boozer, David  17
Boozer, Marie  11, 13, 39, 65, 68, 70, 73, 74, 79, 85, 86, 87
Boozer, Mary Elizabeth  86
Buitenzorg, Java  59

## C

Camp Asylum  9, 27, 29
Camp Sorghum  26, 35, 47
Capers, William "Willie" Henry  33
Carpenter, Captain Emlen N.  48
Charleston, South Carolina  16, 25
Chesnut, Mary  26
Coker, Elizabeth Boatwright  11, 44, 68, 79
Columbia, South Carolina  9, 47, 63
Countess de Pourtalès, the  55

## D

Davis, Burke  86, 87
de Pourtalès-Gorgier, Count Arthur  55
de Pourtalès, Jenny  56, 57, 59, 62, 63, 64
Dickert, David A.  72

## F

Feaster, Amelia  9
Feaster, Ethland  63
Feaster, Jacob  26
Feaster, Jacob, Jr.  22, 53, 54
Feaster, Julia Carolina  22
Feaster, Margaret Narcissa  25, 33
Florence, Italy  58
Frazee, Phineas F.  26, 41, 43

# Index

## G
Gibbes, James G. 29

## H
Harned, Henry or Thomas 16
Holladay, Benjamin 55

## J
Japan 58, 63, 66, 70, 72, 73, 74, 75, 76
Johnston, General Joseph 29
Jones, James Dunwoody 35

## K
Kendrick, Edward E. 49
Krakatoa 60

## L
*La Belle* 12, 45, 46, 52, 68, 79, 81, 84, 85
Lawrence, Robert de Treville 30
London, England 53

## M
Martin, Samuel J. 87
Moore, John Hammond 87

## N
Newberry, South Carolina 19
New York City 42, 52, 53

## O
O'Neall, John Belton 18

## P
Paris, France 53
Pearl, Cora 67
Philadelphia, Pennsylvania 15, 16, 25, 38, 39, 41, 42, 47, 49, 51, 53, 56, 76
Phoenix, Lloyd 53

Preston, Brigadier General John S. 34
Preston, Major William 34

## R
Royster, Charles 87

## S
Sabre, Lieutenant Gilbert 29
Selby, Julian 16
Sherman, John 46
Sherman, William T. 30, 36
Snowden, Yates 69

## T
Toland, Hugh Huger 20

## U
Union League Club 44

## W
Wells, Edward 30
Wittenberg, Eric J. 87
*WPA Guide to the Palmetto State, The* 77

# About the Author

Historian Tom Elmore grew up in Columbia, South Carolina, where he heard numerous tales and legends about life in the city during the Civil War.

Elmore holds a BA in history and political science from the University of South Carolina. He is the author of *Columbia Civil War Landmarks* published by The History Press and *A Carnival of Destruction: Sherman's Invasion of South Carolina*, as well as numerous articles in regional and national publications, and has lectured all across the Mid-Atlantic States. In addition, Elmore is a book reviewer for *Blue & Gray Magazine* and writes the Columbia Gems local history series for *Blue Fish Magazine*. He lives in Columbia with his wife, Krys, and their two Chihuahuas, Speedy and Sassy.

*Visit us at*
www.historypress.net

*This title is also available as an e-book*

www.ingramcontent.com/pod-product-compliance
Lightning Source LLC
Chambersburg PA
CBHW071411160426
42813CB00085B/1068